# *Prayerful*
# WARRIOR
# MOM

# *Prayerful* WARRIOR MOM

## EMBRACING FAITH THROUGH THE STORMS OF YOUR CHILD'S CONGENITAL HEART JOURNEY

TRACY A. RIPLEY

Printed in the United States of America

For more information, email heartmom@prayerfulwarrior.com
Library of Congress Control Number: 2023916477
ISBN: 979-8-89109-210-5 - paperback
ISBN: 979-8-89109-240-2 - hardcover
ISBN: 979-8-89109-211-2 - ebook
ISBN: 979-8-89109-241-9 - audiobook

# GET YOUR FREE GIFT!

To get the best experience with this book, I've found readers who download and use my free *7-Day Scripture Guide* to strengthen your prayer life are able to implement faster and take the next steps needed to have a closer relationship with God.

You can get a copy by visiting:
https://tinyurl.com/7-day-Scripture-Guide

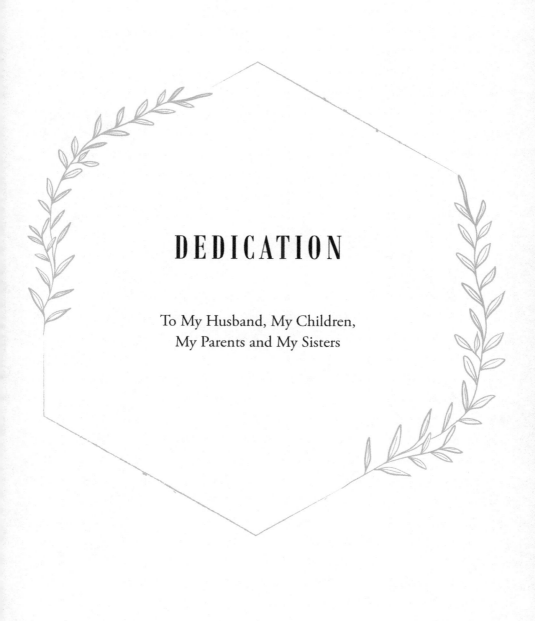

# DEDICATION

To My Husband, My Children,
My Parents and My Sisters

# CONTENTS

# INTRODUCTION

I set out to write this book to share my story with other families going through something similar to what my family experienced. At the time of publishing this book, my husband, Rob, and I will be married for 24 years. During our first ten years of marriage, we enjoyed life as a young couple in a blended family. When I wasn't working or attending night school full time, we were spending quality time with Rob's two older children. Once I graduated and received my bachelor's degree, Rob and I started trying to have a baby together. After three years of trying, fertility tests, and finally leaving it in God's hands, we were blessed with a daughter.

Four years later, I unexpectedly became pregnant with our youngest son. I had a relatively normal pregnancy, with the exception of an intense work environment, and our son was born full-term. I was told my baby had a heart murmur at fourteen hours old. The following hours and weeks would throw my family into a world we had never dreamed of or heard of before—the world of congenital heart disease (CHD). Our son was born with severe aortic stenosis and endured his first heart surgery at five weeks old. While caring for my infant son, I returned to work and fought to keep a career as a working mother, while keeping up with heart appointments, and balancing it all with raising our children to love and respect our Father in Heaven.

This book will take you through years of hurdles our youngest son has had in his young life. You will laugh, you may cry, and you will see how this journey brought me closer to God. My experiences shared in this book are meant to help other CHD families who are finding out for the first time that their child has a congenital condition. When my baby was born with a CHD, I searched for answers and leaned on others who had gone before me to understand what my son's future held. Now it is time for me to give back by sharing our story, so new CHD families will know there is hope for their child to have a full and amazing life. This book is an account of the lessons I learned along this journey as a mother, a child of God, and a working mom. I learned that life doesn't always go as planned, and when I stopped trying to walk alone on my journey and started trusting in God, it was then that I witnessed God raise amazing things out of the ashes of tragedy.

My testimony of faith shared in this book will strengthen the faith of those who already know the glory of God. It will open the eyes of those who want to know Him and are searching for hope. If my story appeals to those who do not believe, and sparks an interest to open your hearts and see His truth, it would make every ounce of sweat, tears, and hard work of writing this book priceless to me.

# PART ONE

# Change of Plans

*"The mind of a person plans his way,*
*But the LORD directs his steps."*

**Proverbs 16:9**

# Angels from Heaven

It was early August 2012. I was working from home because my three-year-old daughter, Reyna, had a wellness visit. This was a time when working from home was more of a one-off privilege than a norm; although my employer had what HR called "flex time," working from home was frowned upon by most managers because many thought working from home meant you were on the golf course somewhere and not actually working. I was quite fortunate to work for a manager who trusted me to work from home. This was as good as gold to a mother of a preschooler with a baby on the way. I was three months pregnant by this time, and life seemed like everything was falling into place.

The year before, I had thrown my hat in the ring to take on a new role at work. It was a stretch role, and the VP of Finance took a chance on me with the caveat that my manager would coach and help me develop the skills I needed to strengthen before leaving me to fend for myself. If I succeeded, I would be the only female business finance manager in the segment. It was both exhilarating and exhausting at the same time. This was my second pregnancy, so I knew I was still in the honeymoon stage.

The first three months were uneventful, except for some mild nausea early on that I did not have with my first. By the third month, I was getting my energy back and embracing this little life that now shared my body with me. I had finally let my manager know I was expecting. I remember stewing over it for weeks, worrying if they would take away the opportunity I had been working toward earning. I vividly remember the conversation. After telling him I was expecting, I asked, "Will this hurt my chances of getting the finance manager position?"

His response was more evidence of the ethical and supportive manager I knew him to be. "If it does, I think HR would have something to say about that."

The phone was ringing. "Darn it!" I forgot to turn the ringer off when I put Reyna down for her nap. I hurried to answer it, not looking at the caller ID. "Hello?" I said rather sharply, irritated that someone was calling during naptime (not that the person on the other end knew that). It was my gynecologist (referred to as my OB in future references).

*How odd that she's calling me and not one of her techs or nurses,* I thought. Then I quickly realized why she had called me directly. The results of my first-trimester screening were in, and she explained the test had returned "abnormal." The first-trimester screening is a combination of an ultrasound of the fetus and the maternal blood screening to identify potential risks for chromosomal abnormalities, including Down syndrome, trisomy 21, and trisomy 18.

My OB explained, "The test can give a false positive and is only one marker used to determine your risk factor and whether additional testing is warranted. While the test combines the ultrasound with the blood test from the mother, it also takes into consideration the mother's age. Since you are thirty-eight, your age could be the cause for the elevated result."

The conversation then turned to her explaining the potential testing available. "There is amniocentesis, which involves taking amniotic fluid from the amniotic sac and carries a risk of potential miscarriage, or a new genetic blood test is available that we could try to run diagnostic chromosome testing. The genetic testing is fairly new and, therefore, is not typically covered by insurance, so you would have to pay for the test out-of-pocket if that is the path you want to choose."

I thanked the doctor for calling me herself and providing the options, but I first needed to talk it through with my husband. I hung up the phone and tried to process everything my OB said. I had been thumbing through a photo album while on the phone, and as I turned the pages, the sonogram from my recent visit fell to the floor. Picking it up, I stared at that picture until tears started burning my eyes. I needed a moment to collect my thoughts, so I headed upstairs to my bedroom.

I didn't even reach the top of the steps when my legs seemed to turn to water, and I sank into a puddle on the staircase, quietly sobbing and trying not to wake Reyna. I opened my fist to unveil the sonogram still in my hand and stared at the silhouette of the angel I had been carrying for three months. I began to pray, *Dear God, please send Your angels from heaven above to watch over my unborn child. Please let this be a false positive!*

I jolted up and went straight to my dresser, where I found the sonogram picture from my first pregnancy. I stood comparing the two. "It is the same baby!" I cried out to God. "They have the same round head, the same button nose, the same tiny hands! Please! You have blessed our family with another child; please grant us Your grace and let our baby be healthy."

My mind was racing, and I started envisioning every possible scenario. Down syndrome was not completely out of the realm of possibilities. After all, I have a cousin with Down syndrome. At this thought, I felt the tension leave my shoulders, and I smiled at the thought of my dear, sweet, kind-hearted cousin. *Yes, Down syndrome is a possibility, but I have seen the amazing, loving person my cousin turned out to be.* I was reminded that if this is the path God chooses for us, He will help us through it.

My husband, Rob, and I already have three beautiful and healthy children. The oldest two, from Rob's first marriage, were the only children we had for the first ten years of our marriage. After attending school at night for seven years, while working a full-time job, when I finally earned my bachelor's degree, we started trying to have a child together. Three years of month-after-month heartache waiting and hoping for a child of my own resulted in the resolution that I was not meant to be a birth mother. I was grateful God had blessed me with the opportunity to be a stepmother to Rian and Kearston (Rob's older two children), and I accepted they would be the only children we had.

In our eighth year of marriage, Rob and I began building a new home together in Northeast Ohio. As our new home began taking shape, I shifted my focus to selecting cabinets, lights, paint, and hardware. Within six months of starting the new build, something else had begun to take shape, and to our surprise, I realized we were finally expecting! This was one of many moments in my life when I learned that patience is having faith in God's timing.

All three of our children had been born healthy and were thriving. Between our two families, our kids have ten first-cousins that were also born healthy and free of any abnormalities. This thought helped reassure me and put my mind at ease. I picked up the phone and called Rob to tell him the results of our first-trimester screening.

◁◇◁◇◁◇◁◇▷

Several weeks later, I was sitting in the parking lot waiting to go into the doctor's office. I was a little early, which was good because I was nervous. Rob and I had decided to go ahead with the genetic testing to give us peace of mind or, if necessary, help us prepare in advance. Rob couldn't get off work since his employer did not pay supervisors for vacation time, so I was going in alone.

I walked into the office and signed my name on the waiting list. Soon they called for me and asked me to wait in one of the exam rooms. *That's odd. I figured this would just be a quick needle stick by a nurse tech, and I'd be out of here.*

A doctor walked into the room and sat down. He began by asking me why I was there.

*Odd question. This is a genetic testing office, isn't it?* I gave him the summary of what I could remember from the call with my OB and explained that we didn't want to risk the amnio test, so we chose this route instead.

Then he dropped the question that rendered me speechless for a moment. "What will you do if the result comes back abnormal?"

My silence must have made him think I didn't hear him, so he asked again, "Would you terminate the pregnancy if the results return an abnormal screening?"

"No. We will be keeping the baby. Our goal of proceeding with this test is to give us answers so we can prepare one way or the other."

I couldn't tell if the doctor was pleased with my response or disappointed. His facial expression was odd, and he simply closed his folder, stood up, and said, "Someone will be in to collect your blood sample."

Now we wait.

The test results would not be back for two more weeks. As I drove home, the doctor's question lingered with me. I was nearly sixteen weeks pregnant, and we would not receive the test results for two more weeks.

*That will put me close to the twenty-week mark or almost five months pregnant! What exactly did that doctor think I was going to do at five months pregnant? I can feel the baby moving at this point. I have heard the heartbeat in parallel with my heartbeat at every exam since my OB confirmed I was pregnant.* Tears streamed down my face. I felt a wave of guilt rush over me for having taken this test.

I knew in my heart that no matter the result, my faith was in the heavenly Father, and I would accept whatever path He chose for me. I prayed for God to help me through the next two weeks while we waited, not to allow worry and stress to overwhelm me.

If there is anything good to say about budget season in the finance world, it is that you do not have much room for worrying about personal things when you are swimming in a sea of intense deadlines and constant demands for reiteration. I was busy meeting with cost center owners who all needed headcount additions and increased spending for research testing, regional leaders who were pushing back on market segment leaders that insisted next year their segment would indeed see double-digit growth rates, and at the same time, funneling the sales demand to the operations team so they could develop next year's production plan. Then, I would roll it all up into a first draft and prepare the slide deck to be reviewed by the business leadership team, only to be told the spending was too high and our bottom line was too low.

The process was a consistent wash, rinse, and repeat until we finally arrived at a budget within our target range. Some of this was new territory for me, and I was more than grateful to have my manager coaching me through the process. I was working more hours as my due date grew near, trying to ensure no loose strings were left while I was off for six weeks. The days and weeks passed quickly, though the thought of the test results lingered and was not too distant from my consciousness. I took refuge in the grueling rhythm of the annual planning chaos because it helped keep my thoughts at bay.

Finally, the day arrived when I received a call from the genetic testing center. I was in a meeting when the call came through, and the message simply asked me to return their call at my earliest convenience. Knowing I was about to receive the answers we were waiting for, I wasn't sure I wanted to call them back while I was still at work. I had already resolved that, regardless of the result, we were keeping the baby, but I was worried that the emotion of it all might be too much for me to contain while at work.

Finally, I got up and closed the door to my office, set my office phone to "do not disturb," and said a silent prayer, *Father in Heaven, please be with me and grant me the strength to endure whatever path is meant for me.*

As the line rang, I was placed on hold while the operator transferred me to the doctor. My hand was sweating as I tried to grip the phone. The last time I got a call directly from a doctor, she gave me the news that landed me here.

I braced myself as the doctor came on the line. "Hi, Mrs. Ripley ... we have received your test results. The screening returned a normal result, meaning we did not detect any abnormalcy in the chromosome testing."

When I hung up the phone, I sat quietly for a moment and then felt a huge release of tension leave my neck and shoulders as I exhaled. I tried to swallow the lump that had risen in my throat. I had mentally prepared myself for the alternative result; however, I could not shake the tears of relief that now welled in the corner of my eyes. The relief came with the realization that I could return to dreaming of all the wonderful things God has planned for my unborn child. Since we were nearly at the five-month mark, I would soon know whether we were having a boy or a girl. I could have found out the sex of the baby from the genetic screening, but I didn't want to take away the surprise of finding out as a family. I already felt like I had let stress from work and anxiety over the genetic testing overshadow the joy of expecting; I was not about to allow another important milestone to be pulled out from under my feet.

⊸◇⊸◇⊸

On a cool fall afternoon in October, I pulled into the parking lot of my OB's office, where I was meeting Rob and Reyna for the anatomy appointment. This is the day we would find out the sex of the baby. Reyna, now four years old, was hoping she would have a baby sister. Once I was signed in, they showed us to the ultrasound room, where the sonogram technician was already waiting for us. I promptly changed into one of the hospital gowns, and then the technician proceeded to get started. She had a bigger screen on the wall that projected the image so that we all could see.

Reyna chatted away as four-year-olds do while the technician went to work measuring the arms, legs, and fingers and was struggling to get pictures of the baby's feet. Every time the technician got close to the feet, the baby would pull away. While the baby was kicking and playing keep-away, she asked, "Do you want to know what you are having?"

We answered, "Yes."

"You are having a little boy."

Reyna continued talking away, and I didn't think she heard what the technician said. I asked her, "Reyna, did you hear? You're having a little brother!"

Reyna didn't miss a beat and replied, "I heard what she said!" and continued right on talking about her gymnastics class as if the lady had just told her the sky was blue.

The technician went on getting pictures and measurements of his heart and lungs and then again went back to try to get pictures of his feet; again, he did not cooperate. The technician laughed and said she had never had so much trouble trying to take pictures of a baby's feet.

We laughed in astonishment as the battle of the feet continued for several minutes until, finally, the technician swept in with a quick snapshot and finally got the pictures she needed. We collected the sonogram pictures we were given of our little bundle of joy and were told that if the doctor saw any issues, we would hear from the office within a week.

On the way home, I asked Reyna, "Why did you ignore the lady when she told us we are having a boy?"

"I heard that lady!" Reyna responded rather poignantly. "I didn't want her to pick a boy!"

Then I finally realized what Reyna meant. She thought the sonogram technician decided whether it was a boy or a girl. "No, honey," I explained, "The lady was only telling us what she saw on the screen. She didn't make the decision. Babies are angels from heaven that choose their family, and our baby chose us to be his family."

I smiled at the innocence of her reasoning. Children take things so literally. I will come to wish I had remembered this in the coming months.

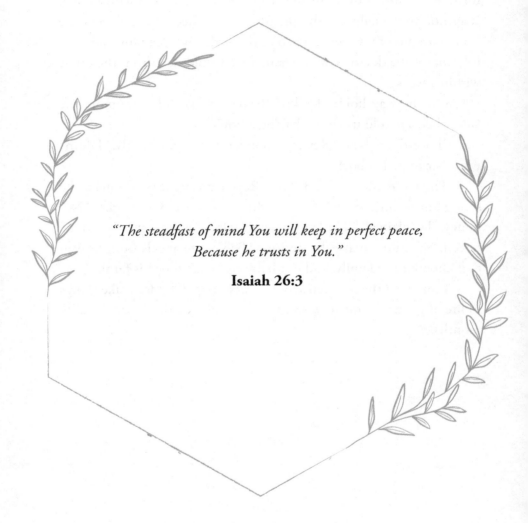

*"The steadfast of mind You will keep in perfect peace,*
*Because he trusts in You."*

**Isaiah 26:3**

# 2

# Grateful for Sisters

It is when we are the most vulnerable and hurting that we see the good in humanity and when our true friends shine. On January 21st, 2013, two feet of snow fell in Northeast Ohio, wreaking havoc long enough to force some interstates to shut down for the day. I was preparing for our global business meeting later in the week and was going over my slides with the person who would be my backup while on maternity leave. I had started having mild labor pains earlier in the day and mentioned it to my friend Cathy, who immediately said, "You should go home or call your doctor."

"The pains have not grown intense enough, and I need to finish walking through the presentation with my backup first."

Concerned for my well-being and knowing the roads were getting bad because of the snow, Cathy called my manager and told him I was in labor and wouldn't go home. My manager, who was attending an offsite meeting that day, called to ask me what was going on. I sheepishly explained to him, "I am trying to go over the presentation with my backup, in case I go into labor tonight." Without waiting for a response, I continued, "I will go home as soon as we have finished, but I am not leaving until I at least provide some notes and talking points. I cannot leave her to deliver a presentation on the fly to a hundred-plus people and not provide her some support."

As promised to my manager, I finished transitioning my notes and went home early from work. I called my doctor's office, and they suggested I try to drink water and put my feet up, as I might be dehydrated. That was a very plausible explanation since I couldn't remember drinking anything but decaf coffee that morning and the thermos of water that I had finished hours ago, but had no time to refill. If it wasn't for the tiny person tap dancing on my bladder, I probably would not have remembered to go to the bathroom. I was always too busy to make myself get up to eat or drink during this busy time at work.

Once at home, I drank a bunch of water and put my feet up, as suggested, and the pains seemed to subside. I was grateful for my friends at work looking out for me—thankful for a manager that put my health and well-being above any presentation, and a friend who didn't take no for an answer. If Cathy had not taken the initiative to call my manager, I probably would have pushed myself to keep working instead of going home and taking care of myself.

The next day, I decided to be on the safe side and work from home, but the pains did not start back up, so I returned to the global meeting the following day. I sat in the back of the meeting in case I had to make a quick exit, and I assured everyone that I was still eleven days too early and I had no intentions of needing any of them to deliver my baby in the middle of the meeting (though some of them jokingly offered). I managed to make it through the day with some mild cramping off and on. I respectfully declined the group dinner outing that evening and went home to rest.

Around four o'clock Thursday morning, January 24th, 2013, I was awakened by fairly intense labor pains. Since this was my second pregnancy, I knew these pains felt more like the real deal this time. They were still reasonably far apart, so I knew I was not in any urgent need to go to the hospital; however, my mind went straight to my budget, which was not yet finalized at work. With the global meeting going on, my focus had been on finalizing the presentations. I thought I had more time to finish the loose ends of the budget. I should have remembered that life does not always stick to your schedule, and things happen when God is ready for them to happen—not when you are.

I quickly started up my laptop and finished loading the last of my budget changes and firing off last-minute emails. Two hours later, I heard Rob's alarm going off for him to wake up for work. I told him, "You should probably stay home today. We may need to make a trip to the hospital."

I called the after-hours number for my OB's office and explained what was going on. They put me on the schedule for eleven that morning and told me to come into the office unless the pains grew significantly worse; in that case, I should go straight to the hospital.

In the meantime, I continued working on my budget, between labor pains, trying to email the final file to my manager. I was perched on my birthing ball with my laptop on the couch, desperately trying to get my file to send, but the attachment was too large, and my computer kept timing out. We still needed to drop Reyna off at preschool before we left, and I still needed to pack her overnight bag for Grandma's house. Time was running out, and Rob's patience was wearing thin. He sternly said, "If you don't get off that computer right now, I am going to throw it in the driveway and run it over with my truck!"

I realized he was right. *What in the world am I doing?* Deep down I knew that none of this mattered right now, but I couldn't help feeling like I couldn't let everyone down at work. I share this part of my story because it is important to understand the level of magnitude I had allowed work responsibilities to take in my life at that time. So much so that I risked potentially giving birth to my unborn child right smack in the middle of my living room. I have always had a very high work ethic, instilled in me by watching my mother work to keep our household afloat after my sisters and I moved in with her during what I was sure my mother would say was the most challenging time of our upbringing ... our teenage years.

My mother, Jane, spent much of my childhood working on the manufacturing floor and wouldn't miss work even if she was sick. If she did get sick, she would vomit, and then go back to work. I recall reaching for my mother's hand when I was young and gasped in shock because of the hard calluses that had replaced her once soft and smooth hands. I would look down at her hands at the hundreds of cuts, blackened by the residue from the braiding machines, and though I knew the answer, I would ask, "What happened to your hands?"

She would laugh and explain, "It is just from the braiding machines at work that sometimes cut me. I can't work with those huge gloves they give us. Don't worry," she assured me, "I can't feel it anymore. My hands are numb to it now."

Though my dad helped with a monthly support check, I was keenly aware that my mom was doing everything she could to keep up with sustaining four costly teenage girls and a house of her own. I always remember feeling a sense of pride in how hard my mom worked to support our five-person family. Until she remarried, we were a house of five women: my mom, older sister, me, and the twins. I learned about credit and why it was necessary by watching my mom fight to establish credit in her own name. Following my parent's divorce, my mom didn't have a loan or credit card in her own name, so she had to start from scratch in her mid-twenties building credit worthiness. I remember when she bought her first car in her own name. I didn't understand why she was so excited about a used car. Then she explained, "Although the car is used, it is the first large purchase I have bought completely on my own, and once I pay it off, I can get a brand-new car because I will have established some credit."

I was proud of my mom when she took on a new job in the warehouse department. Proud to see her challenge herself to advance and also so relieved that her hands no longer were plagued by those calluses. The day I watched my mother sign loan papers for her first home, in her name, I recall thinking, "This is a pretty big leap from that used car loan!"

I am so grateful for the example my mother set for her daughters. She showed us that hard work led to advancement, and advancement led to credit independence. Both my parents instilled a drive in me to want to better myself, to make something of my life. I wanted to make all their sacrifices worth every minute of their backbreaking work, which, I guess, explains why I was now nine months pregnant, sitting on top of a birthing ball in my living room, trying to finish my budget, while breathing through labor pains. I finally resolved to save my budget file into a shared drive on the company network and sent the link to my manager with an email telling him, "I'm in labor and headed to my doctor's office."

Then, of course, I added, "I have my phone with me if you need me."

◇◇◇◇

Later that afternoon, I was anxiously waiting for the epidural to take effect. The labor pains were now one to two minutes apart, and I'd had the needle in my spine for over an hour, but relief had not yet come. My sister Liza, one of the twins, was in the delivery room with us. Liza is the most outspoken of my sisters, and while she likes to tell me she wished she was more like me, it was days like today when I was grateful God made her strong, assertive, and powerfully protective of her family. Liza went looking for some answers.

She returned with the nurse anesthetist, who proceeded to inject medicine directly into my back. He said, "It should start helping in twenty minutes." After which, he was joking around with my sister, and she told him she better not have to come and get him again.

Twenty minutes went by. It did not work.

I had complete numbness on one whole side of my body and the other half still felt every bit of the intensity of the labor pains. The nurse decided she thought my bladder was full (even though I had just gone to the bathroom right before they gave me the epidural), so the next thing I felt was a burning, scraping sensation as the nurse attempted to place a urinary catheter. I heard my doctor say, "That's not good."

And the nurse whispered back, "I didn't think she would still feel it."

My doctor asked, "How long has it been since she received the epidural?"

We said it had been over an hour. She told the nurses, "Get anesthesia back in here to see if they can get her some relief."

However, anesthesia was tied up at the moment. Apparently, another woman down the hall was having the exact same problem, so I would need to wait for them to come and hope the baby didn't decide he wasn't waiting on anesthesia.

Suddenly, the monitor indicated the baby's heart rate dropped. The nurse rushed over and stood watching his heart rate on the monitor; all the while, I was still in excruciating pain and still waiting on anesthesia. My sister asked again, "Is there anything you can do for her?"

The nurse snapped, "My priority is the baby's heart rate right now." She looked at the monitor and mentioned, "Her contractions do not appear on the screen to be as intense as she is indicating." She clearly thought I was over-exaggerating and couldn't take the pain.

Another nurse came in to help. She suggested, "Maybe the device we are using to monitor her contractions isn't working properly."

So they switched it out, and the monitor lit up, indicating that I was having very strong contractions at this point. *Validation!*

I was giving up hope that anesthesia would return in time to give me any relief. Just then, a nurse returned with the guy from anesthesia. He was not joking around this time and actually looked like he felt bad that I was still in a lot of pain. He asked me to sit up because he wanted to adjust the epidural. Since half of my body was numb, Rob and Liza had to help me sit up.

Then the nurse anesthetist said, "I pulled the epidural out about a half-inch."

*Hallelujah, that fixed the problem! Relief! Finally!*

Oh, but not so fast; the nurse now wanted to break my water. The doctor could clearly see that I was not happy about this; thankfully, she said, "She just got some relief from the epidural, let's give her a minute to rest."

*If I could get out of this bed, I would hug that woman!*

The nurse gave me a brief breather, and then she was back to break my water. Now things should move a little faster. After a fleeting moment of rest, I felt the urge to push, but the doctor and nurse were nowhere around. I asked Rob and my sister, "Please, see if you can find one of them."

We pushed the call button, and one of the interns came to check on me. I explained, "I really feel the need to start pushing."

She asked me, straight-faced, "Can you hold it?"

*Can I hold it?* "I didn't say that I needed to pee. Is this some kind of joke?"

The intern ran out of the room and returned with my doctor, who said, "I bet we have him out in three pushes!"

Well, I can tell you it was longer than that because little did I know that both Rob and Liza had pressed the button to give me more pain medicine. Neither of them knew the other had already pushed it, and they both just wanted to make sure that I wasn't in any more pain, so I had started to lose the feeling in my legs. I learned from my first pregnancy that you have to be able to feel something, or you have nothing to push against. They had taken the contraction monitor off my stomach since it wasn't working, but they had to put it back on so they could see when it was time to push again.

After one last contraction and a solid push, I heard the soft, sweet cry of my 8 lb, 1 oz little boy as they placed him on my chest. I cradled my 19.5-inch baby and studied his adorable features. He had blond hair, and he was so still, so calm. I held and kissed his precious face and admired his tiny translucent eyelashes that looked like little whispers when his eyes gazed up at me. His eyebrows were blonde like the rind of a honeydew melon. The thought occurred to me how very different he is from his sister, who came into this world kicking and fighting mad. Reyna kicked and flailed so much when they placed her on my chest, I had to ask Rob to help me hold her because I was afraid she would kick herself right off of the bed.

I've heard that if you have a very outgoing child, your second is likely to be the opposite. I thought, *Maybe this theory is correct, and he will be calm and more laid-back like his dad.* I tried to take in every aspect of this precious baby that I could because I soon had to hand him over to Rob so they could wheel me away for my tubal ligation. The goal was to use the existing epidural in my back so they wouldn't have to give me a spinal if we waited until the next day.

Anesthesia came back again and supposedly numbed my legs all the way to my belly button. I was expected to be awake during the procedure; however, I didn't think the epidural was working quite right again because as the doctor started to make an incision, I said, "Are you cutting me? Because I can sort of feel that. It feels like something is stinging me."

Startled, he asked, "You can?"

The next thing I knew, the doctor was calling for anesthesia, and someone was putting a mask over my face. The last thing I remember was a burning sensation coming from the IV in my hand.

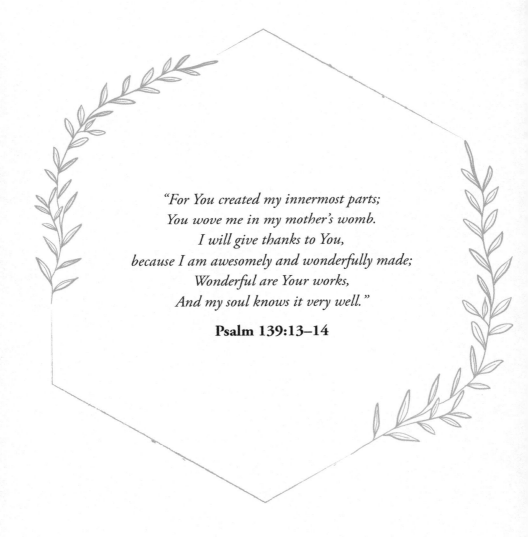

*"For You created my innermost parts;*
*You wove me in my mother's womb.*
*I will give thanks to You,*
*because I am awesomely and wonderfully made;*
*Wonderful are Your works,*
*And my soul knows it very well."*

**Psalm 139:13–14**

# Piecing It Together

I awoke in the recovery room, groggy and shivering. I opened my eyes to Rob sitting next to the bed. I immediately panicked and asked, "Where is the baby? Why aren't you with him?"

"He's in the nursery, getting cleaned up," he said.

The nurse covered me in three blankets and even heated one of them to help me stop shivering. She explained, "It's from the medicine. It should go away when it all wears off."

Finally, they wheeled me to the maternity ward, where I got to hold my baby again. I had nursed him for twenty minutes before they took me to surgery. When I finally got back to the room, he was ready to eat again. Thankfully, with this being my second baby, I knew what I was doing this time and didn't need the lactation specialist to come and help me. We were like pros at this, and the baby quickly settled into a rhythm that very first night of waking me every hour to eat.

Friday, January 25th, started as a quiet day. The roads were still snow-covered, so I didn't have many visitors. Rob had to work and planned to pick up Reyna afterward to come to the hospital to meet her new brother. Early that morning, a nurse had stopped by my room to check on the baby. As she listened with her stethoscope, she said, "Oh! He has a murmur."

Surprised at this, I responded, "He does? This is the first time I've heard anyone say anything about a murmur."

She nodded, "My son had a murmur, and he eventually outgrew it."

By this time, my baby was nearly fourteen hours old, had been checked by the delivering doctor and attending nurses, and no one had mentioned a murmur to me. Later that morning, another nurse came to take the baby to the nursery for a hearing test and to have the pediatrician look at him. Once the testing was completed, she brought him back and said, "He passed the hearing test. The pediatrician will be by to talk to you about his heart murmur."

We returned to the cadence of nursing every hour. Around eleven in the morning, a pediatrician stopped by. "We want to do an echocardiogram [echo] because his murmur sounds more harsh than a regular murmur. It could be nothing," she paused. "But we want to do further testing to determine if it is a murmur that needs to be treated with medicine, or we may want to transfer him to the nearby children's hospital to be monitored," she further explained.

Around noon, they came to get the baby to do the echo. I waited and waited. No one brought the baby back, and no one came to relay the results of the echogram. By two o'clock, I still had not heard anything, and I was becoming quite concerned because it was well past time for him to nurse. Rob and Reyna had arrived to visit. Since the baby was not back yet, they went to get a snack from the cafeteria. When they returned, Rob was pushing the neonatal cribette with our baby in it. "He was just sitting in the nursery when we went by, so I went in and told them I'm taking him back to your room."

⋄⋄⋄⋄

**R**eyna got to hold her new baby brother and visit with me for a couple of hours. The nurses changed shifts at three o'clock, but the new nurse didn't make her way to us until nearly four. When she stopped by, I asked, "Have the results come back from the echo?"

She seemed puzzled. "No one has come to talk to you about that yet?"

I shook my head, "We have not seen anyone. Rob had to go find the baby because no one brought him back to me after the echo was completed."

"Someone from neonatal was supposed to come to talk to you. I really feel they would do a better job at explaining everything to you." She stepped out of the room momentarily and returned holding a piece of paper, which she handed to me.

*Aortic stenosis.*

She explained, "This is what the cardiologist noted in the echo results. I will get someone from neonatal to come and explain it further. They may want to take the baby to the nearby children's hospital to be monitored, but they would be able to tell you that. If they do take him, you can get a pass to go over to see him, and we can have your doctor discharge you early so you can stay over there with him. They have a place there that they allow families to stay if there are available rooms, but if they don't have one available, we can let you stay at this hospital and have security drive you over to visit." Then she turned and left.

I looked at Rob. "They want to take him."

"What makes you think that?"

"Why else would she go into such detail about me staying there, and why would she tell me what I could do if they don't let me stay if they are not already considering moving him? It sounds like she already called my doctor to see about getting me discharged early. Doesn't that seem odd to you?"

A few minutes later, the nurse returned with someone from the NICU. He explained the baby was born with aortic stenosis; the valve was too small, and he gave us the impression that it would require open heart surgery. Then he apologized and said, "I thought we were further along in the process than we are. I thought the pediatrician had explained everything to you. I'm sorry, the transport team is here to pick him up."

I interrupted, "Wait! What? Are you telling me they are here to take him ... now?"

"The transport team is in the hallway," he said matter-of-factly. "We will give you ten minutes to say goodbye." He turned and left the room.

At this point, I was doing everything I could to hold it together and not lose it in front of Reyna, but the lump in my throat was becoming too much to bear, and the water in my eyes too persistent. I held my baby in my arms and didn't want to let him go. I just kissed his sweet face and held him so tightly as the tears I could no longer hold back ran down my face. I turned to Rob, "Do you want to hold him before they leave?"

I kissed him one more time before handing him to Rob. It felt like mere minutes before the transport team was in the room to take our baby away. Things seemed to spin now. Reyna was asking, "Why are you guys sad? Why are Daddy's eyes red?"

Neither of us could muster up words to answer her because any attempt to do so might erupt into full-blown cries of despair.

The transport team handed me a soft, cotton handkerchief covered in pastel hearts and polka dots that someone had sewn one corner to look like a doll's head with a long nightcap on top. They said, "Sleep with it tucked under your shirt tonight, and we will place it in the incubator beside the baby. It will smell like you and comfort him."

I wasn't sure if that was true or more of a way to offer me some small fraction of a job, so I could feel like I was doing something for my baby while I was separated from him. Maybe it was both.

The nurse returned to my room to take some blood from me. "We need it in case they need to give the baby any blood."

"Why are they taking your blood, Mama?" Reyna asked. "Will they have to take mine too?"

The nurse assured her she wouldn't need to give any blood. Then the nurse gave me some Q-Tip swabs. "You can use them when you pump your breastmilk. Swab whatever you can get on the Q-Tips, then seal it in the vials. Since your milk has not come in yet, this will ensure the baby can get all the colostrum from you because it is full of antibodies. The Q-Tips will be sent to the children's hospital so the NICU nurses can swab the baby's mouth with them."

"How am I supposed to feed my baby if we are in separate hospitals? I have already started breastfeeding him, and he was doing really well."

"We will give him a bottle with your breastmilk when it comes in."

I was absolutely against that. "He is not even twenty-four hours old yet; I don't want him to get nipple confusion and mess up all the great progress we have already made."

"We can use a feeding tube instead," she said.

I started getting choked up and was trying not to cry again. "No! I don't want him fed through a tube!"

Someone popped their head in the room, said they had the baby ready to go, and asked if we wanted to say one last goodbye. Though I was walking through what felt like a dream, I slowly made my way to the hospital room doorway. There my baby lay, in a portable incubator.

Reyna immediately started asking questions. "Why did you put my brother in there? Where are you taking him? Are you going to bring him back?"

I tried to open my mouth but could not form any words. I couldn't muster my voice enough to answer her or to ask her to please stop asking questions. I think Rob or someone on the transport team may have answered her. I was in a fog.

*This can't be happening!* I couldn't believe it.

I left the side of the incubator and wandered back into the room, trying to find clothes to change into so we could go over to the children's hospital to see our baby. As I turned from gathering my clothes, Rob grabbed my arm and pulled me close to him. We stood together, holding each other and crying until we were interrupted by someone bringing my dinner tray.

I asked her to take it away because I had lost my appetite. My nurse had followed her into the room and told me, "You need to eat."

"Fine. Leave it."

The nurse came back to talk to me about the feeding tube. She said, "If you are worried about nipple confusion, it would be the best option. It would allow you to breastfeed, and they will use the tube to supplement until your milk comes in."

I turned to Rob, "Let Reyna eat the dinner tray they brought. She needs to have her dinner anyway, and at least it won't go to waste."

A little while later, the phone rang. A NICU nurse asked, "Are you okay with the feeding tube?"

"Yes," I agreed.

She replied, "Good. Otherwise, we would have to start an IV."

The NICU nurse said they would be ready for us to visit in about an hour. This gave us time to let Reyna eat and for me to get myself ready. I hung up the phone and lay on the bed, my face buried in the pillow. All I could think about was them putting an IV in his little arm or how they would get a feeding tube in his tiny body.

With all the commotion, I had forgotten about my incision from the tubal and was painfully reminded of it now as I struggled to get dressed.

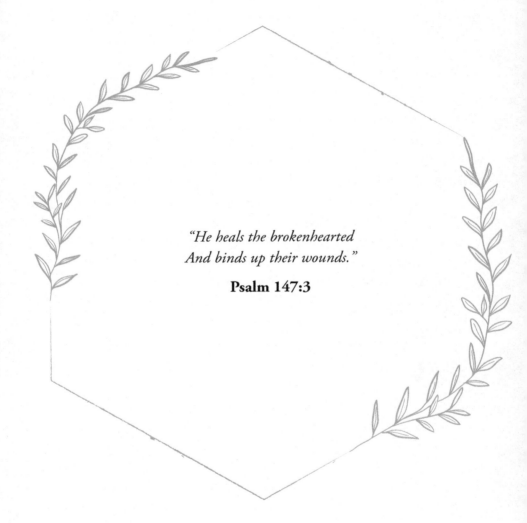

*"He heals the brokenhearted
And binds up their wounds."*

**Psalm 147:3**

# 4

# No Bridge Between

My eyes searched the room full of incubators, filled with tiny newborns, for my son. This NICU did not have individual rooms for each baby. Instead, there was one giant room with sections divided only by curtains. Four babies were in the area where my baby was being monitored, and I quickly found him. He was not difficult to find because he was the only baby in the room that weighed more than five pounds. He was also the only baby without a name. I walked to his bedside, and there, on his name plaque, read "Baby Boy Ripley." Rob and I had been going back and forth between two names and had not yet finalized the paperwork with the name we had chosen before they transported him, so there my baby lay—nameless. It broke my heart again. I don't know why it was so important at the time, with surely more pressing questions that needed to be answered, but I wanted his nameplate updated as soon as possible. My baby has a name, and it is Bryce.

The NICU nurse noticed us and walked over to introduce herself. She saw me staring at the countless wires they had all over my baby and explained they had what they call "leads" on him. The leads were little tabs stuck all over his chest that monitored his heart rate and breaths per minute, and a pulse ox on his toe measured his blood oxygen level. Every so often, they would put a blood pressure cuff on Bryce's leg to monitor and track blood pressure levels. It took my breath away to see my baby like that.

The nurse tried to reassure me by telling me, "He is sleeping and is nice and comfy," but all I could think about was how I had held him in my arms only a couple of hours ago, free from wires. Now here he is in this incubator where I have to ask the nurse to help me if I want to hold him or if I can put my arms through the holes in the side of the incubator to touch him through thin rubber gloves. My heart was breaking.

I kept telling myself he was in good hands and that the doctors would not have him here if they did not think it was necessary. While we were visiting, they came to do an electrocardiogram (EKG). They had to peel off all the leads on Bryce's chest to put on different ones (twelve of them) to do the EKG. The leads were stuck to his skin so severely that Bryce cried when they pulled them off. It irritated me to see that they had put one over his nipple. *How painful that had to have been when they pulled it off!*

His little chest was not big enough to fit all twelve leads, so they put some on his arms and legs, but they fell off when Bryce kicked or moved. The nurses and I had to hold the leads on while they took the EKG. Around 9:00 that evening, the doctors were making their rounds. All the specialized doctors, attending physicians, and head nurses came around to each patient to get a status update for the shift change. One of the heart doctors talked to Rob and me about Bryce's condition. He explained, "Aortic stenosis is when the valve between the lower left heart chamber and the aorta is narrowed and doesn't fully open. This reduces blood flow from the heart to the rest of the body. We want to monitor Bryce's levels to ensure he is strong enough to go home. Bryce will need a balloon surgery to open the valve, but we need to determine when the surgery will be done. The longer we can wait and allow him to grow, the bigger he will be, which would improve the outcome of the balloon cath."

I had to be back to my room at the other hospital by 10:00 p.m., so we had to say goodbye for the night. The hospitals were only across the street from each other, but there was no bridge between them like many of the neighboring parking decks had connecting the hospitals. Rob went to get his truck while Reyna and I walked to the lobby to wait for him. I was really beginning to feel the full effects of my surgery because of all the walking. I wasn't supposed to be standing so much following my tubal, and I had refused the Percocet my nurse offered before we left the hospital because I was worried it would affect my breastmilk. She had given me some milder pain medication instead, but it had worn off hours ago. Since we had not prepared for having to leave my hospital room, neither Rob nor I had any Advil or Tylenol with us either. My stitches were killing me, and my incision was seriously aching. I was trying to breathe through the pain and hold back tears.

When Reyna and I reached the lobby, a sign on the doors said they were closed after 9:00 p.m. and directed us to use the other door, exiting to another street. I didn't recognize the street name where it had said to exit, nor did I realize it was just off to the right. All I knew was I was in pain and couldn't walk any further. I started mindlessly talking out loud. "Great! Now, where do we go? I can't walk any further! How are we going to get out now? How did Rob get out?"

Then Reyna snaps me back to reality. She's panicked now. "Does the sign say we're trapped in here?" she innocently asked. "I don't want to be stuck in here. How do we get out?"

I thought I had noticed Rob's truck pull up outside. I sat on a bench and told Reyna, "See if Daddy is standing outside around the corner." Then I realized that I just sent my four-year-old daughter to open a door, and I wasn't really sure if Rob was standing there or if it was a stranger! I immediately started trying to stand up and walk, as quickly as my body would allow, to catch up with Reyna.

I turned the corner to find her pounding on the glass doors, yelling, "Help! Help us! We're stuck in here!"

I saw Rob pointing at the door (it was locked), so I pushed the release and it opened. I had tears streaming down my face. Rob looked at the two of us perplexed, and Reyna proceeded to tell him, "We were trapped in here."

I tried to explain the confusion about the doors and how I was in pain. He helped Reyna and me back to his truck and drove me back to the other hospital. It was getting late, and Reyna was falling asleep.

"Rob, I don't want to make Reyna walk all the way back to the maternity ward to drop me off. She is so tired, and it is well past her bedtime."

He pulled up to the main entrance and said, "Wait in the truck." He went inside.

He returned with a security guard who put me in a wheelchair to take me back to my room. I said goodnight to Rob and Reyna and sadly watched as they drove away.

✧✦✧✦✧

In my room in the maternity ward, my nurse smiled, "I got a hospital-grade breast pump for you, and I put some sandwiches in the fridge in case you're hungry."

"Thank you for doing that," I said. "I'm not hungry, though." My eyes were so tired, and I was in excruciating pain.

"Do you want a Percocet for the pain?"

When I protested again about it affecting my breastmilk, she assured me, "It is safe for breastfeeding mothers to take."

So I agreed. I desperately hoped it would knock me out, so sleep would take me away from reality for just a little while. As I stood in my hospital room, I could hear the babies' cries in the rooms surrounding mine. All I could think about was the fact that I was surrounded by other moms who had their babies, and my baby was taken from me and placed in a completely different hospital. They are bonding skin to skin, and my only connection to my baby will be through a doll-like handkerchief I was supposed to sleep with pressed against my skin. I just wanted to sleep and escape the sounds of all the other moms and their healthy babies.

My nurse returned with the Percocet and explained how to use the hospital breast pump. Then she said, "I will come back in three hours to wake you up to make sure you pump."

I lay on my bed praying, *Father in Heaven, please bring sleep to my eyes quickly. Please take this ache from my heart and send Your healing angels to watch over my son. Help the doctors and nurses to care for him as I would and let him know he is loved. Please, God, let sleep come quickly...* and I softly cried myself to sleep.

⬦⬦⬦⬦

As promised, my nurse came in at 1:00 a.m. to wake me to pump. At this point, all I got out was the colostrum, so we put it into syringes. "They will put the syringes in the baby's feeding tube and use the Q-Tips to swab his mouth." She helped me label the Q-Tip swabs. "It will be shift change soon, and I will be going home. I will explain everything to your new nurse and have her wake you at 4:00 a.m. to pump again," she assured me before she left.

At 4:40, a nurse tech came to check my vitals, and I startled awake when I saw the time. "I was supposed to pump at 4:00 a.m.!" I exclaimed.

She was just there to take my temperature and wasn't my new nurse. Clearly, my new nurse would not be as helpful as the last one, so I set my alarm to wake me at 7:00 a.m. After jolting awake and attaching myself to that monster machine of a pump (that latched onto you like you were in a heavy-duty vise grip), my mind would not slow down long enough to allow sleep to return. I didn't need my alarm anymore. I lay awake thinking about my baby, who seemed a world away from me right now. I searched for that paper the nurse had given me and I typed "aortic stenosis" into my search engine.

For the next three hours, I lay in bed reading through tears all the information I could find about what caused this issue in my baby's heart. I read through countless articles trying to understand if anything I did or didn't do during my pregnancy caused this. I had been under so much stress throughout my entire pregnancy between the genetic testing, the constant chaos at work, and not drinking enough water or moving enough throughout the workday. I recalled reading an article about green tea during my first trimester that said it could cancel the effects of folic acid from prenatal vitamins. After reading that, I completely stopped drinking any type of tea, but still questioned one midwife at my OB's office during a prenatal visit whether I should be concerned about what the article had said.

The midwife said it was fine to drink, but I cut out all green tea anyway. Now my thoughts returned to that article. I blamed myself. All I wanted to do right now was get out of this hospital so I could be with my baby. I still needed to see my OB to examine my incision so she could release me.

While waiting to be discharged, I showered and packed my things. The hospital photographer stopped by while I was in the shower and left a note that she had missed me. I was glad that I had missed her. I didn't want to have to speak the words out loud, "My baby isn't here. He is in another hospital, so he can't have his picture taken."

Finally, my OB stopped by to check on me. I explained everything that had happened and that I was trying to secure a room at the other hospital so I could stay there tonight.

"If you can't get a room there, you can stay here, but we can't provide you with meals or medicine."

That gave me some comfort because at least I had a backup plan and wasn't worrying about not being close to Bryce tonight or finding a ride in the morning since I was not yet released to drive.

My new nurse came to check on me a little later. She informed me, "You are essentially discharged, but I won't enter it into the computer until you figure out what you are going to do for the night.

I am working until 7:00 tonight, so you have plenty of time to figure it out." Then she called security and let them know I needed a ride over to the children's hospital.

I walked downstairs to the main lobby, and a security guard was nice enough to drive me over. She took it easy on all the bumps on the way over (which I would learn to appreciate more after my ride with security the next day). That night, I could not obtain a room at the other hospital. I needed to get on the list before noon, and we had missed the window. I would stay at the hospital where I gave birth so security could drive me in the morning.

Since I needed to return to my room before my nurse left at 7:00 p.m., we had to cut our visit a little short today. Rob and Reyna took me back to my room to help me get settled and ensure I could, in fact, stay. Once I was all set with my room for the night, they would head home. We all needed a good night's rest. Since I was technically discharged, I walked them to the parking deck to kiss them goodbye.

I stood in the doorway, watching them walk to the truck in the darkness, with Reyna holding her daddy's hand and skipping by his side. I wanted to run to them … to go home with them. I felt so conflicted because my heart ached to be with them at home, but I knew my obligation as a mother was to be here for my baby. I felt so incredibly disconnected from my newborn child. My ability to bond with him had been stripped away, and when I did go visit my baby, I had to ask someone to help me with all the tubes and wires so I could hold him. I had to set reminders on my phone to remind me to use a breast pump because I was not allowed to nurse my own child.

I walked back to my room and fell asleep that night with the TV on, attempting to drown out the sounds of the mothers with their healthy babies in the rooms next door. Laying in bed, I prayed for a bridge to carry me to my children in their dreams, to let them know they are not alone because my love is forever with them as long as they live.

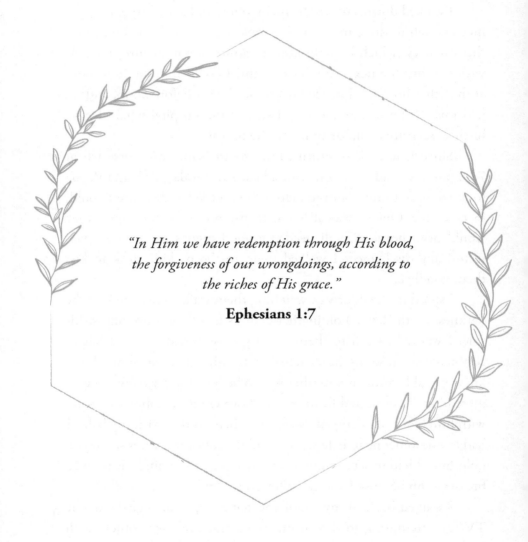

*"In Him we have redemption through His blood, the forgiveness of our wrongdoings, according to the riches of His grace."*

**Ephesians 1:7**

# 5

# God's Grace

The room was quiet, with only the purr of the monster machine breaking the silence as it tugged at me. I read you should make the area around you as quiet and calming as possible when using the breast pump because stress and anxiety can affect your milk production. I was using the hospital-grade pump made available to nursing moms of the NICU and PICU patients of the children's hospital. It was hard to make yourself feel calm with a machine squeezing your lady parts in a vise grip. I closed my eyes and tried to think of my infant son, who was still lying in an incubator in the NICU. My milk had finally come in, but the nurses were still combining it with formula and feeding Bryce through a feeding tube.

They had a required amount of ounces per feeding, and if I didn't get enough when I pumped, the nurses would supplement the rest with formula. For instance, their schedule said he needed three ounces of formula every two hours, so if I only pumped two ounces, they would supplement one ounce of formula through his feeding tube. I was told we could not take Bryce home until I produced enough milk to meet their feeding requirements. Each day, when I would think I finally hit their required levels, I would be told that the level had increased. I was becoming progressively frustrated with the situation and could feel the heat in my face burn as my frustration grew to anger.

I was blessed with two strong and supportive father figures in my life. David, my dad and biological father, taught me how to fight (both physically and verbally). He taught my sisters and me to be strong, assertive women, and he taught us to face our fears. While he was raising four girls, he never put limitations on what we could do in life. He didn't raise us to think that way. "You can do anything in life that you set your mind to."

We carried logs; we helped dig the family garden and brought tools from the garage while he lay beneath his car on the asphalt driveway shouting, "Bring me the 3/16 wrench!" We practiced karate in our living room as he taught us how to defend ourselves, and he made us climb to the roof of the house to hand him shingles, even if we were afraid of heights. His number-one rule when we were growing up was to stick up for ourselves and our family (you saw this earlier when Liza was passionately protective of me).

Once, when a boy in the neighborhood kept knocking down Rachel (the other twin) by kicking her knees out from under her, my dad told us if Rachel came home one more time with a bruise on the back of her knees, he was going to whoop us all for not sticking up for our sister. The next time the kid kicked my sister, he was the one that went home crying. While my dad's methods may have been unconventional, the lessons were clear: you don't sit idly by and allow anyone to walk all over you or someone you love.

My stepdad, Jerry, came into my life when I was a freshman in high school. He received a bit of a rude awakening when he met my sisters and me. We would be fist-fighting and arguing with each other one minute and crying, stomping off, and slamming doors the next. He had raised boys, so teenage girls, especially four girls who didn't take crap from anyone, were a whole new world for him. I still say it was a blessing from God that he didn't run away after the first time he watched one of us stomp through the house, mad as hell, and then come back half an hour later, smiling and laughing. He would look at my mother and ask, "Is that the same girl that just came through here?"

My mother would laugh, "Yep! Welcome to the world of teenage girls."

One hot summer afternoon, I was push-mowing the grass when my stepdad came home. A family friend was in the house talking and laughing with my sisters. He had been visiting most of the day. I was just finishing up the lawn and walked into the house behind my stepdad. My face was red as a turnip, and I was a sweaty mess. The sun was never kind to my fair skin. I noticed my stepdad seemed agitated, but I didn't have any idea why. I later learned that he was angry with our family friend. He explained, "I was not raised to sit by and allow a friend, certainly not a woman, to push mow two acres of grass in 102° heat index while he sat in an air-conditioned house."

My stepdad was teaching me respect—for others and, more importantly, for myself. With the men in my life, I had the best of two worlds that helped shape me into the person I needed to be today. One man encouraged me to stand up for myself and fight with conviction when someone hurt me or my family, and the other taught me to take a step back to look at the big picture in a situation and recognize when something was just not right. These character traits would serve me well, and I attribute my willingness to advocate ferociously for my children to the lessons my fathers taught me.

I knew I was in unchartered waters with having a baby with a heart condition, but this was not my first rodeo with caring for or nursing an infant child! Something finally pushed me to my brink, and I'd had enough! I felt that fire in my stomach urging me to *stand up ... speak up!*

Then another voice told me not to get myself kicked out of the NICU.

Finally, I asked Bryce's nurse, "Why are you holding a breastfed baby to standards for a formula-fed baby?"

She pulled one of her co-workers over to talk with me. "We need to ensure he is eating well before he goes home because, for heart babies, eating is like exercising, and they can tire out and refuse to eat."

"Okay, I get that," I said and further argued, "Bryce getting tired from eating shouldn't dictate that he should be fed more ounces than what he would normally eat if he were strictly a breastfed baby. Formula and breastmilk are not the same consistency. When I nursed my daughter, she ate more frequently because breastmilk is digested faster than formula, so breastfed babies will eat smaller meals but more frequently."

We were standing near Bryce's bed, and I felt like I wasn't getting anywhere when one nurse saw a NICU doctor walk by and asked if she could stop over. The doctor asked, "What's wrong?"

I explained my concerns. "At the rate I am going, I will soon be producing enough milk for two babies because they are holding us to the levels a formula-fed baby would be eating."

This is one of many of what I like to call "moments of God's grace" that happen throughout our story. I once heard a sermon my pastor gave about God's mercy and grace. I used to think they were similar, but as my pastor explained, "God's mercy is withholding something we deserve [i.e., withholding punishment], and God's grace is bestowing a blessing we do not deserve." Psalm 86:15 tells us, "But you, Lord, are a compassionate and gracious God, slow to anger and abundant in mercy and truth."

God knew we were all born sinners, and through Jesus Christ, who died for us on the cross, He showed us His mercy when we did not deserve it. Grace is a blessing, a gift undeserved:

> "For God so loved the world, that He gave His only Son, that everyone who believes in Him will not perish, but have eternal life" (John 3:16).

We, as sinners, deserved to be on that cross at Calvary, but God bestowed a blessing upon us we did not deserve: His forgiveness of our sins. *This is grace.* This is love.

At the time, I didn't understand that it was God who intervened to help me, but as my story unfolds, you will see that this happens quite often. It took me a few years to recognize it and even longer to learn to listen when He calls for action on my part.

It just so happened that the doctor the nurse had summoned over to our conversation had breastfed all three of her children, understood my concerns, and agreed Bryce should not be held to formula-fed standards. In defense of the NICU nurses, I will add that the doctor explained, "The NICU nurses are not accustomed to having a baby that could nurse. Look around you," she said. "Most of the babies we treat are premature and too tiny for their mother even to hold them to nurse. Some premature babies have thin, transparent skin that is too delicate or sensitive to touch. The NICU nurses don't know how to measure exactly how much milk the baby is getting from you. They are used to being able to track precisely the fluids going in and coming out. Since Bryce is a heart patient, we are also monitoring his heart function according to how much fluid he drinks and how much he expels."

As a compromise, the doctor asked if we could all agree to remove the feeding tube and allow me to nurse my baby. The nurses could weigh him before eating and again afterward. The weight change would be the amount he ate. *Finally, I would get to hold and nurse my baby again!* What are the chances that a woman doctor would walk by at that moment, and what are the odds that she had nursed all three of her children?

The answer: God's grace.

Over the next few days, I continued to stay at the hospital so that I could be there to feed Bryce every two hours. I was permitted to stay in the family housing area meant for out-of-town families with patients in the NICU (similar to a Ronald McDonald house but for short-term stays). The only exception was the first two nights when I stayed at the hospital where I gave birth and one other night when another family with a child in critical condition needed the room.

On the night I could not use the short-term family room, they would not permit me to stay by Bryce's bed in the NICU, so I went home with Rob and Reyna. It was nice to be home with them, to sleep in my own bed again, but at the same time, my heart ached to be with my baby. I had to set my alarm for 1:00, 3:00, and 5:00 so I could pump to ensure that my body kept up with Bryce's feeding cycle. Then I had to sleepwalk downstairs to label and place the milk in the freezer. It made me grateful for the room on the nights that I was able to stay at the hospital. It provided a sufficient place to sleep and shower and allowed me to be right down the hallway so I could get up at night to nurse him.

Waking yourself up with a phone alarm to nurse your baby does not provide anywhere near the same motivation as having a crying baby wake you from sleep. On at least two occasions while staying at the hospital, I slept through my alarm and woke to the phone in the room ringing. It would be the NICU nurse calling to ask, "Are you coming to feed him, or should we just go ahead and give him a bottle?"

*Give him a bottle? They know he is a breastfed baby, and I have strictly asked them not to give him a bottle! What is she thinking!?* This was enough to have me flying out of that bed, half asleep with my hair a mess and my pupils still trying to focus in the fluorescent lighting. Thinking back, she may have known that was exactly the motivation I needed to get my butt down there because my baby was hungry!

*Thank You, God, for Your grace.*

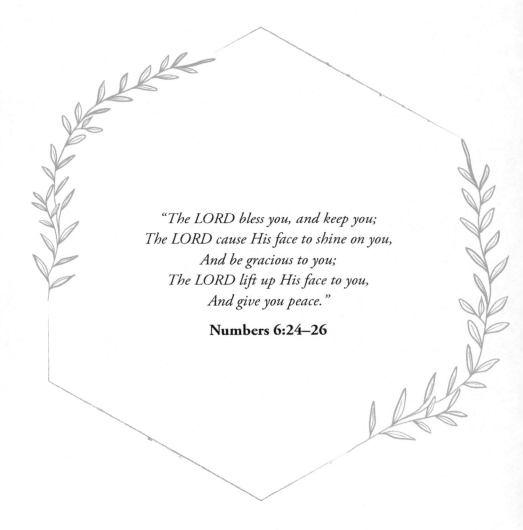

*"The LORD bless you, and keep you;*
*The LORD cause His face to shine on you,*
*And be gracious to you;*
*The LORD lift up His face to you,*
*And give you peace."*

**Numbers 6:24–26**

# Change of Schedule

On January 29th, Bryce was released after five days in the NICU on the condition that I would bring him to see the cardiologist every other week for check-ups; on the off-weeks, I would take him to see his pediatrician. I agreed to these conditions, and with his first heart appointment scheduled one week out, I packed up my baby in his infant car seat and headed home.

On my way, I called Noah's Ark, the daycare where Reyna was for the day, to tell them Bryce had been released and that I'd like to pick her up on our way. I was fully expecting to leave the car running and just pop inside to get Reyna because we were supposed to be extremely careful about exposing Bryce to any germs or the flu. With it being January, flu season was at its peak, so this would surely be a challenge.

I pulled into the daycare parking lot and saw Reyna standing on the sidewalk with Miss Shauna, waiting for us. Miss Shauna was the sweetest, most loving teacher at Noah's Ark, and she took it upon herself to get Reyna bundled up and ready so that I did not have to leave Bryce in the car or go inside the daycare.

As I looked at Reyna standing on the curb, anxiously waiting for us, I could see the effects the last week had had on her too. Her eyes had dark, deep circles under them due to lack of sleep from staying late at the hospital, visiting with Bryce and me, and then getting up early every morning with Rob to take her to daycare while he went to work. The long days and short nights had taken their toll on us all, and Reyna was not exempt from the exhaustion we felt. Seeing her smiling face waiting there as we pulled up filled my heart with gladness that we would all finally be home together at last.

Once Rob found out Bryce had been discharged from the hospital, he left work early and met us at home. He helped carry Bryce's car seat into the house since I was still not quite healed from my surgery. Rob sat the infant seat on the living room floor, and Reyna ran straight over to hug and kiss her newborn brother. Rob stopped her. "Go upstairs and change your clothes first."

She headed up the stairs.

"And make sure you wash your hands too because you were at daycare all day, and you can't get Bryce sick right now," he hollers as she's headed upstairs to change.

⊰◈⊱◈⊰

The next day, when Rob came home from work, he said that his dad, Bill, had to go to the hospital because he was having difficulty walking. He couldn't pick up his legs. We had only been home one day from the NICU with Bryce and were being cautious about not taking him in public, so taking him to the hospital right now was not a good idea. Rob was receiving updates from his mom, Kathryn, about how Bill was doing. They had been running a lot of tests all day, so his dad was pretty tired and not really up for visitors this evening anyway. We were all still reeling from a week of anxiety and lack of sleep, so we agreed we would wait to see if they were keeping him before we made plans to visit.

The next couple of weeks were as normal as any other family with a newborn. I was getting up every two hours to nurse. The one large difference was that my body had grown accustomed to the production level the monster machine at the hospital forced me to produce, so I had more milk than Bryce would eat in one sitting. I would have to feed the baby and then pump for twenty minutes. By the time I got everything packaged, labeled, placed in the freezer, and cleaned up, it was time to feed the baby again. I was told it might take a little time for my body to sync up with the baby and soon I would only produce what he demands. In the meantime, we were stockpiling what many moms refer to as "liquid gold."

Our first visit with the cardiologist was one week after bringing Bryce home from the NICU. After an EKG, a blood pressure check, and a physical exam by the cardiologist, they sent us to the cardiac sonographer for an echo. This was the day I learned what was different about Bryce's aortic valve. The sonographer explained, "Bryce's aortic valve is considered a bicuspid valve, which means that it only has two compartments instead of three."

He further described it: "A normal aortic valve is shaped like a Mercedes symbol. A bicuspid valve is shaped like a football. This is why Bryce's heart has to work so hard to push the blood to the rest of his body." The tests taken during the echo would measure what they call "the gradient" of the blood flow through the valve. Bryce's gradient ranged between 40 and 50 and would peak at 60.

After the echo was completed, the cardiologist met with me and said, "Everything was the same as when Bryce left the hospital—not better, not worse. However, you shouldn't allow him to cry or get really worked up. That will make the gradient peak, and the closer it gets to 70, the more critical it will be to do something to help lessen the gradient. I would like to wait to do anything until Bryce is at least six weeks old to allow his lungs to be fully developed. Then we will schedule the balloon heart catheter as an outpatient surgery."

For now, the plan was to stick to every other week, and in-between, I would take Bryce to the pediatrician. That way, he would be seen by a physician every week. Once the echo was completed, I went to scheduling to make our next appointment. The lady in scheduling said the cardiologist was unavailable for three weeks, so she pushed our next heart appointment out for three weeks instead of two.

I did not know she had not asked the doctor if he approved of pushing the appointment out for a week.

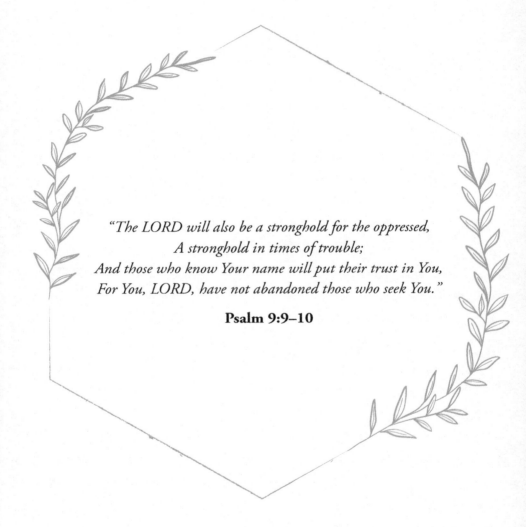

*"The LORD will also be a stronghold for the oppressed,*
*A stronghold in times of trouble;*
*And those who know Your name will put their trust in You,*
*For You, LORD, have not abandoned those who seek You."*

**Psalm 9:9–10**

# Going Home

I hate the smell of hospitals. After living in the hospital for a week, I didn't expect to be returning to that smell so soon. It smells like a mix between Clorox and Pine-sol to me. There truly is something to be said about the association between memories and smell because as soon as that smell hit me, my mind was right back in the NICU with Bryce. It made my stomach twist into knots.

Reyna ran ahead of us to be the first to push the button to the elevator. I shouted from behind her, "Don't touch it! It's filled with germs!" I caught up to her to use the sleeve of my shirt to press the elevator button. Reyna scoffed at me that she wanted to push the button. I reminded her, "We have to be careful not to get Bryce sick, and elevator buttons are a breeding ground for germs." The elevator stopped at the third floor, and we stepped out to search for the room number Kathryn had sent to us. Bill was still in the hospital. He had been diagnosed with lung cancer, which had spread to his back. He had tumors in his back that had grown so large they were pinching a nerve, which is why he couldn't pick up his legs.

The hospital had started an aggressive round of radiation treatments to shrink the tumors. Since Bill couldn't come to the house to meet Bryce, we decided we would take Bryce to meet him. We were still extremely cautious and covered the infant carrier with a blanket while walking through the hospital. We had a huge bottle of hand sanitizer in the diaper bag, which we all used after touching any doors (or the elevator). Reyna also did a great job policing people who wanted to hold the baby. She would present them with the Purell bottle, followed by a mini-lecture. "You can't touch Bryce with germs, or you will make him sick!"

We didn't stay too long on this first trip to see Bill. I was still nursing, so I'd have to get Bryce home to feed him soon. I was never one of those moms who could hold the baby, cover myself with a shawl, and manage to discretely feed the baby in a public place. I had a horrendous fear that I would drop the shawl trying to adjust the baby and inadvertently expose myself to a bunch of strangers. So I tried to keep close to home and make our trips short.

Bill was in good spirits and happy to see us when we walked into the room. He had a lot of wires hooked to him with all the medicine they had him on. We asked if he wanted to hold the baby, but he said he was worried he'd drop him because the radiation was making him weak. So, Rob held Bryce up to his dad so he could see the little boy who now shared his middle name. Reyna showed her papa the hip-hop dance moves she learned in dance class and asked him when he was coming home.

"All I want is to be able to walk again so I can go home," he replied.

The doctors had told him the cancer was too advanced, and they would try to get him to a point where he could go home to live out his last days. It was likely he would only live another year. We were fortunate to make two more trips to the hospital over the next couple of weeks to visit my father-in-law before he took a turn for the worse.

⋄◇⋄◇⋄

Late Sunday evening, February 17th, Rob's phone was quacking. He has the strangest ringtones on his phone. I tried to find it before it woke the baby. "Hello?"

"Hi, Tracy, it's Kathryn. Is Rob there?" She sounded tired, and her voice was shaky.

I handed Rob the phone and told him it was his mother.

Bill was now at a nursing home. They moved him there the previous weekend to help with physical therapy while he underwent his last radiation treatments. Kathryn had noticed Bill was having trouble breathing. She persisted until the nursing home finally took him back to the hospital, where they took a CT scan and MRI. The hospital found that Bill's colon had torn, and he was becoming septic.

Kathryn asked Rob, "Could you come to the hospital?"

Rob knew it must be serious for her to ask him to come so late. We could not find someone to babysit under such short notice, and I couldn't stay long anyway because I'd have to come home to nurse, so I stayed home with Reyna and Bryce while Rob went to see his dad.

Hours later, I was still sitting up, waiting to hear something. The house was dark and quiet when I heard the garage door open. It was after one in the morning. As soon as Rob moved into the light, I could see the solemn look on his face. "What happened?" I asked.

"They had to take my dad into surgery to clean out all the septic fluid that had seeped from his colon. They told my dad it was urgent, and he would not make it through the night if they did not do the surgery right away. Dad protested he had four more radiation treatments and needed to do those first. We finally convinced him that this surgery was critical and needed to be done first," he paused. "The surgeon pulled me aside and said we should say what we wanted to say to Dad now. He didn't know if Dad was strong enough to survive surgery."

The family was permitted to see Bill and talk to him before they would take him back to surgery. Rob's sixteen-year-old daughter,

Kearston, was allowed to go back to see her papa and read him a letter before they took him to the operating room.

The next morning, Rob called his mother to find out how his dad was doing. Bill made it through the surgery, though he was on a ventilator and had a ton of tubes and IVs going into him. Rob and I went to the hospital the following day to visit. Bill was in intensive care, and they wouldn't allow Reyna back to see him, which was okay with me because I didn't want her to see him like that, anyway. Kathryn stayed in the waiting room with Reyna and Bryce while we went back to see Bill. When we walked into his room, Rob's eldest son, Rian, was there, visiting with his papa. We waited to give him some time with his grandpa, and then we told him his grandma was waiting with his brother and sister in the lobby.

As I approached Bill's bed, I was stunned to see a man who had just been walking around, smiling and laughing, just three weeks ago. A man who had helped Rob build our house only four years ago. To see him lying in this bed, immobile and attached to countless wires, was heartbreaking. He couldn't talk to us but could hear us and would respond by nodding.

When we were leaving, Bill held up his arms and waved at us. I leaned over, kissed him on his forehead, and whispered, "We love you."

⋄⋄⋄⋄

February 20th, 2013, we were at the JC Penney's Portrait Studio, a place that received way more of my discretional spending than I care to admit. The photographer knew us so well that she was kind enough to schedule a time slot in the least busy hour to limit any potential exposure for Bryce. Bryce was now three weeks old; his last echo appointment was two weeks prior. This was the week we were originally told to go back to the cardiologist, but the next heart appointment was a week away because of the scheduling conflict.

Instead, as promised, I had scheduled an appointment with the family pediatrician to examine Bryce and check how he was doing.

During the photo shoot at Penny's, I noticed Bryce breathing a little funny. It only happened a couple of times (that I had noticed), and I chalked it up to maybe he was getting tired because it was close to his naptime. That evening, I mentioned it to Rob and asked if he had noticed it too. Now, I was seeing it more frequently. Bryce would breathe, and his whole body would lift up, shoulders and all, as if trying to take a big, deep breath. Sometimes, his breathing would get faster.

The next day, I took Bryce to the pediatrician, mentioned the breathing thing I had noticed, and asked if it was anything to worry about. While we were in the pediatrician's office, he also noticed the sporadic deep breathing that Bryce was doing, where his shoulders would raise as he breathed. The doctor said, "It is just something babies do. Babies don't have a rhythm established, so they sometimes breathe very fast or even so slow that it scares parents into thinking they've stopped breathing."

I had recalled Reyna doing that in her sleep sometimes when she was an infant, so I accepted that as a plausible explanation. We returned home thinking nothing was wrong and returned to our normal routine.

As the week moved on, Bill started slipping. His kidneys had started to fail. The doctors were now discussing a life plan with Kathryn and Rob's sister. They wanted to know, "How long do you plan to leave Bill on the ventilator?" If there was no improvement soon, they would have to make a very difficult decision.

That day came on Monday, February 25th. One by one, the machines were turned off, most of the IVs removed, and Bill was made as comfortable as possible. He became very still, and his breathing slowed as time passed by silently until the moment the Lord called him home.

"Stop striving and know that I am God;
I will be exalted among the nations,
I will be exalted on the earth."

**Psalm 46:10**

# Walking with God

**Y**ou are officially a mother once you've been christened by the warm, slimy spit-up from your baby. On this particular day, Tuesday, February 26th, 2013, I was being baptized in it. Bryce started spitting up after he finished nursing. At first, it was minor and didn't seem cause for concern; although, it first happened after I had eaten a peanut butter sandwich and later nursed him. I suspected it was possibly an allergic reaction, so I cut out anything with peanuts from my diet, but the spit-up got worse. In fact, it was to the point where I had to place towels all around us when I fed him, because anything within three feet of us was within target range. So I called the pediatrician and explained my concerns.

That evening, I received a voice message from the doctor telling me to bring Bryce into the office the next day. So I took Bryce back to the pediatrician's office and explained everything that had been going on. I said, "This just started yesterday morning. We haven't had any issues with vomiting like this before when he nursed."

"It sounds like he has acid reflux. Although, it is odd because typically, babies that have acid reflux have it from the moment they are born. When is his next heart appointment with the cardiologist?"

"He has one scheduled for tomorrow."

"Good," he said. "I feel better knowing Bryce will see the heart doctor tomorrow. Make sure you keep that appointment and be sure to go."

*I have every intention of going, so that seems like a silly thing to say to me.*

I took Bryce home again, and the vomiting slowed, but so did his eating. I lay beside the bassinet that night, listening to my baby sleep. He was making this funny noise while he slept, the sound you make if you hold your breath and softly grunt. I could not sleep listening to him breathing like that. I took my phone out and recorded him because I wanted to play it for his doctor the next day.

There, beside his bed, I prayed over my infant son. *Father in Heaven, thank You for the blessing You have bestowed upon my family with our newborn son. I don't know what is wrong with him, and I ask You, please, Father, place Your healing hands on my son and help us get through this night until we can see the heart doctor in the morning. My husband is already grieving the loss of his father, whom we lost only three days ago; please don't take our son too. I pray that You will watch over Bryce and help him to live a long, healthy, normal life. I ask this in Your name, Jesus. Amen.*

**I** dropped off Reyna at Noah's Ark on Thursday, February 28th. Originally, she was not supposed to attend daycare while I was on maternity leave. Since the heart appointments lasted over two hours sometimes, it was too long to ask Reyna to sit quietly. It also made it difficult for me to hear what the doctor was saying because she was normally chatting and asking questions, as four-year-olds do. The daycare agreed to let her attend one day a week when Bryce had doctor's appointments.

Rob had already left because he needed to leave work early today. He was meeting his mom and sister at the church to discuss Bill's memorial services with our pastor. At the heart doctor's office, we walked through what had become normal procedures: EKG, blood pressure check, physical exam, and then the echo. While the cardiologist was completing the physical examination, he asked, "Have there been any changes to Bryce's health since you were here last?"

I then explained the two trips to the pediatrician over the last two weeks and that his pediatrician had not been concerned. The cardiologist was not aware of either of these visits and seemed concerned that the pediatrician had not notified his office of either visit. He said, "We will talk more after they finish the echo."

When the sonographer was finished, he stepped out of the room and returned with our heart doctor. The cardiologist reviewed the pictures as he talked with the sonographer, but I could not hear what they were saying. Finally, the cardiologist turned to me and said, "We need to admit Bryce to the ICU right away."

I was stunned. *We were supposed to schedule his balloon cath when he's six weeks old,* I thought. I wasn't prepared for this at all. Immediately, a million thoughts were flying through my head, and I was trying to listen to what the doctor was saying, but my thoughts were drowning him out. *What would this do to Rob? How could I tell him this now after he just lost his father? What would we do about the funeral services? Who is going to pick up Reyna? What is going to happen to my baby?*

I started talking faster than I could think. "This is horrible timing. This was supposed to be a scheduled procedure," I reminded him.

He calmly replied, "Remember, I explained to you that we would wait as long as Bryce's heart tolerated it. He is very sick. Your son needs medicine."

"I don't understand how this could happen!" I said, choking back tears. "I took him to the pediatrician twice! I thought something was wrong two weeks ago, but he kept sending us back home. Rob's dad passed away on Monday," I pleaded. "I can't even call Rob right now because he's with his mother and our pastor planning his father's memorial."

The doctor looked at me with the most serious expression and spoke in a very intense tone. "You and your husband do what you have to do and take care of what you need to take care of. Your son will be here in good hands, but he needs to be admitted right now!"

This is a man that is soft-spoken, calm, and is referred to as the "baby whisperer" by everyone who knows him. He has never spoken to me this way. I could see the intensity in his demeanor. He motioned for me to move closer to the monitor where they had taken pictures and video of Bryce's heart. He asked, "Do you remember when you were here last time, you could see Bryce's heart pumping on the monitor?" He motions with his hand like he's squeezing a Nerf baseball, mimicking the rhythm of the heart. He then pointed to the monitor and said, "This is Bryce's heart function today."

I looked at the screen. The motion of the heart on the monitor is pulsing ever so slightly, barely visible, a mere flutter on the screen. The gravity of what he was saying finally hit me. My voice cracked as I tried to steady my lip from quivering. I whispered the question in fear of his response, "Is he going to die?"

"He is very sick, and we need to get him medicine so his heart can get to a level to sustain surgery."

I was trembling now. I misdialed Rob's number three times before I finally heard the phone ringing on the other end. "Can I call you back?" Rob asked.

I was silent for a moment. I tried to steady my voice so I could speak. "They are admitting him."

I did my best to explain what was going on without sobbing on the phone. Rob started asking the same questions I had asked about scheduling the surgery. I told him, "They said it can't wait. Bryce needs medicine right now."

"I will pick up Reyna and come to meet you."

Next, I called my mother and told her what was happening. She offered to keep Reyna so Rob could come and be with Bryce and me. I let Rob know my Mom would pick up Reyna and gave him a list of things I'd like him to bring to the hospital, the most important being my breast pump. Bryce hadn't eaten since before we left the house, and I was getting uncomfortable. They didn't want me to feed him if he had surgery in the morning. I turned back to the cardiologist and told him, "I'm staying with Bryce."

"A nurse will be by to walk you to the PICU."

The heart doctor's office is across the bridge from the children's hospital, and the nurse said, "You can carry him to the PICU floor." I felt like my shoes had suddenly turned to bricks, and I couldn't get one leg to pass the other. We began crossing the bridge. It felt like such a long walk. I didn't even see the people as we passed by them. The only thing I knew how to do right then was pray. It gave me the strength to pick up my legs and move my feet closer to wherever this path was leading me.

Praying has always calmed me. It makes me feel closer to God and reminds me I am not alone in this world. As we walked, I began my silent prayer, *Father in Heaven, my son needs You right now. Please remain by our side and give his heart the strength to endure until he can get the surgery he needs. I beg of You; please don't take my son! I have waited so many years to finally have children of my own; please, don't take him from us now. I ask You, Jesus, to please take my prayers to the Father and petition upon our request for His mercy and grace.*

The nurse led me to a staff elevator down a long corridor. I was not paying attention to what floor we were on. I was still praying as we walked.

"Our Father, who is in heaven, Hallowed be Your name. Your kingdom come, Your will be done, on earth as it is in heaven. Give us this day our daily bread. And forgive us our debts, as we also have forgiven our debtors. And do not lead us into temptation, but deliver us from evil. For thine is the kingdom, and the power, and the glory, forever. Amen" (Matthew 6:9–13).

I didn't even realize we had finally arrived on the PICU floor, and the nurse was motioning for me to step into one of the rooms. She told me to place Bryce in the infant hospital bed. I stood there, holding him and kissing his face. I didn't want to let him go. Finally, I relinquished and laid him down.

Suddenly, the nurses were popping in and out of the room, trying to get an oxygen cannula placed and ID bracelets on us both. The nurse who walked me over had disappeared, and new nurses were asking, "When did he last eat? When was his last bowel movement?"

A different doctor came to see Bryce. He was also a cardiologist and worked in the cath lab. I had to reiterate everything that had happened the last two weeks all over again to each nurse or doctor that came to see Bryce. The doctor from the cath lab explained, "The procedure that Bryce needs is a balloon heart catheter, also called balloon valvuloplasty. We will go through an artery in Bryce's leg to his heart and then push the balloon through the aortic valve, inflate it, and pull it back through to force the valve open. The flaps in Bryce's heart valve are sticking together, and there is only a very small space at the bottom of the valve where the blood can get through. The first indication that Bryce was in heart failure was the labored breathing two weeks ago." I could tell he was agitated that the heart doctors had not been notified that Bryce had a breathing issue or had been vomiting when eating.

He continued explaining the risks of the cath procedure and the risks related to anesthesia for such a small child. Next, I was told, "We need to set a PICC line in Bryce's leg. It will be used to administer critical medicine that he needs. We will use this same line in the morning to do the balloon heart catheter procedure, so getting it in tonight will help save time and provide a port to administer the epinephrine drip. The epinephrine will help get Bryce's blood pressure and heart function to a sustainable level for surgery in the morning. We only have one chance to get the line into his leg tonight. If the nurse can't get it in one try, we will wait until the morning when Bryce is in surgery. If we keep trying in that vein, it will blow the line, and then we would not be able to get the catheter in to do the balloon inflation."

I agreed to let the nurse try to do the PICC line that night. Rob arrived at the hospital, and the nurse, who had arrived to set the PICC line, asked, "Do you want to stay in the room and watch while I set the line?"

I didn't want to make her nervous with something so critical, and I honestly didn't want to watch my baby get poked with needles, so I went to the waiting room with Rob to update him on everything I had been told so far. As we waited, I said a silent prayer, *Please, God, watch over my baby. Help him get the medicine he needs to help his heart improve for surgery in the morning. Please don't leave our side, dear Lord.*

The nurse appeared in the doorway to call us back to the room.

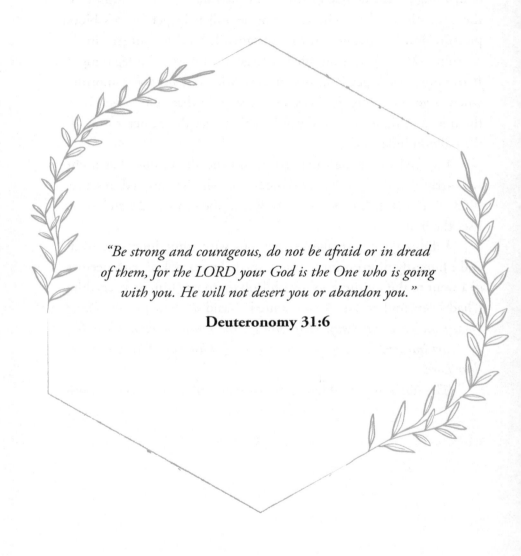

*"Be strong and courageous, do not be afraid or in dread of them, for the LORD your God is the One who is going with you. He will not desert you or abandon you."*

**Deuteronomy 31:6**

# This Is Not Where It Ends

R ob and I walked hand-in-hand toward the hospital room where our five-week-old son lay. He now had a line attached to an artery in his left groin. The nurse was successful in getting the line set on the first try. *Thank you, Jesus!* I silently prayed as I approached his bed. The tube led to a bag on an IV pole beside the bed. The pole had three different medicine monitors on it, one of which was the epinephrine, and one looked like saline for fluids. They had placed the tiniest nasal cannula in his nose to help boost his blood oxygen levels.

"Given Bryce's condition, he will be first to receive the heart cath, so someone will probably be by to get him at 7:00 a.m." his nurse told us. Since he was scheduled to have surgery first thing in the morning, he was not allowed to eat. Another gut-punch—the one single thing that I could do at this moment to help my son, and they wouldn't let me feed him. It was heart-wrenching every time I held Bryce; he would turn toward me as if he was ready to eat. I kept having to shift sides or sit Bryce up because he could sense me and start rooting. He knew it was time to eat and was getting angry because I wasn't feeding him. The nurses suggested placing blankets between us, but Bryce was not fooled. He knew the milk was right there, and he'd cry because I couldn't feed him.

Rob had gone home to be with Reyna. He was still working on writing the eulogy for his father's memorial services on Saturday, and we both agreed it would be best for Reyna to sleep in her own bed tonight. As the night waned on, we no longer needed to put blankets between us because Bryce stopped rooting and no longer cried out in hunger. He was still as he lay peacefully in my arms, so quiet and so calm as I prayed over him, sang to him, and kissed his face and tiny hands. I held him so long in the rocking chair next to his bed that my arms were going numb. The nurse offered me a pillow to put under Bryce to help bear the weight, because I didn't want to put him down. I didn't want to let him go.

As it started to get close to two in the morning, my eyes were growing heavy, and I had drifted off to sleep, sitting up in the chair and still holding Bryce. The nurse asked, "Do you want to put Bryce in the bed?"

"No."

"You need to get sleep yourself. You will need your strength for tomorrow."

She was right; I would be of no use to Bryce tomorrow if I didn't try to sleep. I thought maybe she was also worried I would fall asleep and drop Bryce on the floor. I finally conceded, and placed Bryce in his little bed. The nurse brought me some blankets and another pillow for the fold-out futon bed in the room. Well, it was shaped like a futon couch, but it was more of a hard pleather sofa. I wasn't complaining because, at least, I was allowed to stay in the room with him twenty-four-seven on this floor. I tried to lie down and rest my eyes, but anyone who has ever tried to sleep in a hospital knows it is no small feat.

⋄⋄⋄⋄

Every time a monitor beeped, I would sit up to ask questions to find out what was happening. One particular alarm sounded exceptionally louder than the others, and when it went off, Bryce's nurse would yell, "He's bradying!" and another nurse would come running in to help.

Once things had calmed down, I asked, "What does it mean when you say he's 'bradying'?"

"Bryce's blood pressure is improving, but every now and again, it will drop extremely low, which made the monitor start sounding an alarm."

I anxiously watched the clock. I prayed, "God, please just let my baby make it so they can help him." I kept thinking, *We just have to make it to seven in the morning.*

The room was dark, with only the occasional break in the silence coming from the monitors and the glow from the medicine monitors casting a faint light in the room. I couldn't sleep. I sat against the back of that pleather couch, watching the stillness of my baby sleeping. There was a peacefulness in the room. Bryce and I were alone, though I did not feel alone. I felt God's presence around us, and remembered my mother's words when I called her earlier that evening. "It's going to be okay, Tracy."

Her words reminded me that my son needed me to be strong, so I took a deep breath and continued praying for strength and peace to get us through the night. I thanked God for the blessings in all of this, from the first nurse, who wasn't even my normal nurse, who came in to check on Bryce at fourteen hours old and detected his murmur. If she had not had a son with a similar murmur, and had not heard Bryce's murmur, where would we be today? Bryce would have been in heart failure, and we would not have known what was happening. He would not have seen his cardiologist today, who sent us to be admitted.

I recalled God's help with the nurses in the NICU and sending the doctor to us, who had nursed her three children. If she had not been the doctor to be walking by at that very moment, Bryce might have never left the NICU. We would not have had the last couple of weeks together at home as a family, and my milk production would have been over the top if I had continued trying to meet the requirements of a formula-fed baby. Then, earlier today, God again extended His grace to us when He sent the nurse to set the PICC line. Bryce needed that critical medicine to help his heart improve for surgery, and she had one chance to get it right. I felt God's love all around us.

> "Come to Me, all who are weary and burdened, and I will give you rest" (Matthew 11:28).

God's love and protection warmed me like a soft blanket and gave me peace to drift off to sleep, slumped over on the couch until I was awakened at six o'clock by the x-ray team. They had come to take x-rays to ensure that Bryce's heart was getting more stable for surgery. I quickly got myself dressed, relieved the tightness in my chest with the breast pump, and ran down to the cafeteria, hoping to be back before the doctors made their rounds.

⊰⊱⊰⊱

When I returned, the nurse said, "You just missed rounds. They said Bryce has shown improvement from last night, and his blood pressure is better."

This was somewhat reassuring, but my bubble was soon popped when a lady came to talk to me from the cath lab. She greets me, "So we'll be seeing Bryce at four o'clock today in the cath lab."

I practically jumped out of my seat. "What? No way! He was scheduled to be first today!" I demanded. The lady looked confused as I proceeded to tell her, "This is unacceptable!"

As she left, she told me, "I will look into it."

After three hours of broken sleep, the adrenaline rush caused by a lady telling a mother her son will have to wait to receive the surgery he needs was enough to snap me awake better than any stiff cup of coffee. I was angry. I was confused and scared. *I thought we just had to make it to seven in the morning. How could they ask us to wait nine more hours? It had to be a mistake.*

Just then, my older sister, Tina, walked into the room. I was so incredibly relieved to see a familiar face but also confused because I didn't know they would let her back to see us. I soon figured out that they didn't let her … she came back on her own. It wasn't long before the nurse came in and told her, "Only parents and grandparents are allowed back here."

My sister told her, "I'm just checking on my sister. I will wait in the waiting room." Tina continued to stay and talk to me as I filled her in on everything that was happening.

The nurse returned and told Tina again that she had to leave. My sister sternly told her, "I'm going." She visited with me for a few minutes more and then retreated to the waiting room of the PICU floor.

I told you … my sisters and I look out for each other. It's what has been instilled in us since childhood, and when one of our own is in need, we will fight fiercely to help them.

A little while later, Bryce's nurse comes in the room and apologizes for having to make my sister leave, but "It's just policy," she said.

"I understand, but under the circumstances, she is the only family I have to lean on for support right now."

"Why is that?"

"My father-in-law passed away on Monday, so my husband and mother-in-law are busy helping with funeral arrangements, and my parents can't come up because they are helping watch my four-year-old daughter," I explained.

"I will talk to patient support to see if there is anything they can do to allow her to come back to be with you," she said.

Soon the patient support lady showed up and basically told me there was nothing they could do … "It's policy."

A little while later, Liza also came to the hospital, so I went to the waiting room to visit with them briefly, then returned alone to be with Bryce.

⋋⋋⋌⋌

I was sitting in the rocking chair, holding Bryce, watching the hands on the clock tick by. The cardiologist I met yesterday when Bryce was admitted to the PICU stopped in the room. He said, "We are having staffing issues in anesthesiology, which is the cause for Bryce's surgery being pushed back. I talked to the cath lab and got Bryce's surgery moved from four o'clock to noon."

I was still not allowed to feed him, though, because they needed to prep him for the noon surgery. I looked at the clock … three more hours. I gazed at Bryce's sleeping body. He was so still and quiet. I was trying to remember the last time I heard him cry. My eyes began to burn as tears threatened to push through. I tried to recall Psalm 34:18, "The Lord is near to the brokenhearted and saves those who are crushed in spirit."

*Do not be afraid,* I reminded myself; *God is with us.*

More doctors came. The chief cardiologist of cardiac surgery talked me through a list of what seemed like never-ending potential risks or problems associated with the surgery. I was asked to sign that I understood and agreed to the procedure anyway. Then, someone from the cath lab came … more risks and potential issues.

*I wish they would just stop telling me all these bad, possible scenarios. What choice do I have in the matter? The alternative was to do nothing, and my baby will die! Why load my mind up with every possible risk or worry?*

Time lagged on … noon came and went, and no one came for Bryce.

❖❖❖

**A**t one-thirty in the afternoon, Rob walked into the room. My shoulders relaxed in relief. I was still holding Bryce and praying over him. I began updating Rob about everything I knew. He went to find the nurse and check to see what was going on. Finally, a man from anesthesia came to see us. He went through an entirely different set of risks or potential complications. This time, at least Rob was by my side to lean on for comfort and support. Before leaving the room, the man looked me straight in the eye and said, "I have three boys of my own. I will treat your child as if he is one of my own. It will take about half an hour to get Bryce under. I don't want you to sit and worry, so I will come to the waiting room to let you know as soon as I get Bryce under the anesthesia."

The lump in my throat came back.

❖❖❖

**W**e were waiting in the hallway behind Bryce's hospital bed, which was finally headed to the cath lab. It was three in the afternoon now. A large family was blocking the hallway, with little kids and several young-looking adults standing around another child's room. *Maybe the patient advocate had a change of heart, and there is hope they will let our family back to see Bryce later,* I thought.

They finally all crammed into the room so we could pass by. Rob and I walked beside the bed as we moved further down the hall until the bed came to a stop near a set of doors that read *Cath Lab. Staff Only.*

I bent down to kiss Bryce's tender cheek. I whispered softly in his ear, "I love you," as I let go of his tiny hand. They pushed the bed through the doors of the cath lab, and I stood there watching as my baby was wheeled further and further away from me until he was out of sight. I prayed to God, *Please let me see my son's precious face again.*

Just then, the words of Carrie Underwood's song, "See You Again,"[1] began playing over and over in my mind. In that moment, I felt comforted that God was telling me this is not where Bryce's journey ends. As I stood there watching my infant son being wheeled into heart surgery, I had an overwhelming sense that I would, in fact, see him again.

---

[1]  Carrie Underwood. "See You Again." BMG Rights Management, Kobalt Music Publishing Ltd., Warner Chappell Music, Inc., 2012.

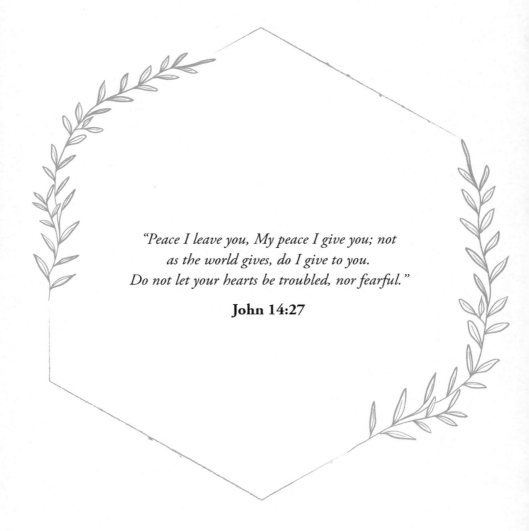

*"Peace I leave you, My peace I give you; not as the world gives, do I give to you. Do not let your hearts be troubled, nor fearful."*

**John 14:27**

# 10

# No Time to Grieve

My family waited in the waiting room as my infant son's balloon heart surgery was still ongoing. I had to excuse myself to go pump, so I walked back to Bryce's room. I tried to ignore the hospital bed that now sat empty in his room. I went straight to getting myself ready to pump. At least this helped me feel closer to my baby. I could close my eyes and convince myself I was doing something to help him during a time when I felt absolutely helpless.

As I was finishing labeling all my bags of liquid gold, Bryce's cardiologist came into the room. He looked very serious. I couldn't read if he had good news or bad. He explained, "They were able to open the valve, and the pumping chamber had a positive reaction."

*This is good news,* I thought.

Then he continued, "Bryce is doing good. I wanted you to be prepared that he is going to come back intubated and will remain on the ventilator for several days. We need to let Bryce's body have a chance to get used to the new anatomy and also give his body some time to rest after how long it had gone with having to work so hard. They will be finishing up soon, and someone will come to the waiting area to talk with you. I just wanted to be sure you knew that the balloon cath did what we needed it to do."

Two and a half hours after I watched my son wheeled into the operating room, one of the cardiologists who had performed the balloon cath procedure came to talk to me and my family in the waiting area. "The surgery was successful. We are already seeing improvement in the heart function. With these types of procedures, we try our best to limit the amount of regurgitation, or leakage, caused by the balloon cath, and we would have liked for Bryce's leak to be smaller, but it is doing what we needed it to do."

When the doctor stood to leave, I turned to my mother, who was sitting beside me, collapsed my head on her shoulder, and buried my face in her arms. "Thank God!" I cried.

Breaking the tension, my sister Liza said, "Damnit! I should have been sitting there! That was my shoulder she should have been crying on!" She always knows how to make me laugh.

My older sister, Tina, looked at me and said, "It sounds like he may need more surgeries when he's older."

I looked at her, puzzled. "Did he say that?"

"The doctor said Bryce may require additional surgery when he's older, but time would tell how the leak progresses," Tina said.

Apparently, I had not heard anything the doctor said after he told us the surgery was successful. That is why, I learned, it is important to take someone with you to doctor appointments when you are receiving serious news or instructions. Four ears are definitely better than two!

❖❖❖❖

As I walked into the hospital room, I had to catch my breath at the site of Bryce lying in this tiny hospital bed with more wires going into his little body than I could count. It was overwhelming. The cardiologist had warned me that he would be on a ventilator and still sedated, but nothing could prepare a mother to see her infant connected to so many wires and have a machine breathing for her baby. They had moved the PICC line to his right groin now. They removed the line in his left groin from the night before. The one that was placed on the right today was used to lead the cath up Bryce's artery to inflate the balloon in his aortic valve. The nurse that had kicked my sister out earlier had agreed to allow my sisters and parents back to see Bryce after his surgery.

Right away, we all noticed that Bryce's left foot and leg were swollen and purple. We asked the nurse about it, and she said, "It is normal. It should go down in about two hours after surgery."

A little later, the other cardiac surgeon, who also helped perform the balloon heart cath surgery, came to check on Bryce. Liza mentioned to the doctor, "We are concerned Bryce's leg is still really swollen. It has been well over two hours since his surgery."

The doctor looked at Bryce's leg, then looked at the clock. He called the two nurses over and asked, "Why is he laying flat like this? I had him elevated! Why isn't he covered up? Why isn't this on?" he shouted as he banged his hand against the overhead heater.

One nurse said, "I put the bed down when x-ray came in to take pictures, and I must have forgotten to put the bed back up when they finished."

The doctor scolded them. "Get him elevated! Cover him up! And turn this heater back on!"

Another blessing from God that Liza asked about Bryce's leg when she did. We were told later that if his circulation continued to be stressed like that, he could have lost his left leg. The nurse who forgot to set the bed back up happened to be the same nurse that had given Tina a hard time about being in Bryce's room. She was much nicer to us after that.

The cardiologist continued answering our questions and was very patient in explaining what Bryce's future might look like.

"Will Bryce need more surgeries in the future?"

"It mainly depends on how Bryce's body and heart do as he grows older. Some people go many years without having any secondary surgeries until they are much older. With medicine constantly changing, the older Bryce gets, the more options he will have," he explained.

Liza asked, "Will Bryce be allowed to play sports when he's older?"

"He will probably never be able to play coached sports."

I honestly wasn't worried about whether Bryce could play sports at that moment; I was grateful God saved him and that he had a future to look forward to. Twenty-four hours ago, I didn't even know if my baby was going to live.

The cardiologist told us, "Medicine has already come such a long way in terms of understanding these types of cases and also finding ways to treat them. Babies born forty years ago, with the severity that Bryce has, would have died. Even if they had known how to look for a bad valve at that time, they didn't have the technology to treat it. Most babies born with aortic stenosis were just told they had a heart murmur. If they had the severity that Bryce has, they passed in their sleep. Their death would have been ruled SIDS [sudden infant death syndrome] simply because they didn't know the baby had a bad valve."

❖❖❖

**I** awoke in the hospital room. When I opened my eyes, I had to focus for a minute to remember where I was. I had stayed up half the night watching Bryce. He was quiet and relatively peaceful through the night. Sometime around three in the morning, I had fallen asleep and had the best three hours of sleep I'd had in days. It was Saturday, March 2nd, 2013; I remembered that Bill's memorial services were today, and I had to go home to get ready. I gave Bryce's nurse my cell phone number and told her to call if there were any issues and that I would be back later that evening.

I drove home in a fog and found Rob sitting in the recliner, trying to finish his eulogy. His eyes were red and tired. He told me he didn't know if he could read it without crying. "So what if you do cry?" I said. "Your dad passed away. If someone thinks you shouldn't cry, then they are pretty insensitive! I will read it for you if you want me to, but I really think it would mean more if it comes from you."

At Bill's memorial services, we greeted people and thanked them for coming. I saw faces and shook hands, but I felt numb. I felt like I was walking through the motions, but my brain was on autopilot. Rob read the tribute about his dad's life. He talked about the funny stories they had as he was growing up and said, "I appreciated everything my dad did to provide for our family. As a kid, we never moved around a lot. We had what we needed and never went without. The one thing my family always had growing up was laughter, and I am thankful for those memories. My dad taught me the importance of working hard for the things I earned in life, and I only hope that I will leave that same legacy when I pass."

When he finished, it was my turn to say a few words about Bill. I had written my thoughts down at the hospital but left my paper on the table at home so I would have to talk from memory. I know God helped me through that speech because everything in my memory at that time seemed to be mush. I told a story of a time when we, as a family, went out to eat for Rian's birthday. It was a Mexican restaurant, and Bill had ordered fajitas. They were the kind they bring to your table on a hot plate, and you're supposed to assemble them yourselves. The waitress came back to check on us and asked Bill if everything was okay.

He said, "Yes, everything is good."

"Are you sure? If you don't like it, I can get you something else."

Bill insisted that he liked it and was fine. When the waitress walked away, we looked over at Bill to see why she had been making such a fuss and found that Bill was eating all the toppings separately instead of building the fajita. We laughed and told Bill how he was supposed to eat it, but he replied, "Naaaww! I like it this way! It's good!"

I explained, "I told this story to illustrate the way my father-in-law lived his life. He was happy with the simple things in life. He took pride in the things he earned through hard work. He loved his family and would do anything for them and loved spending days with his little chihuahuas and his Massey Ferguson tractors. Many of you know that Rob and I welcomed a new addition to our family recently. I have been so heartbroken knowing that Bryce would never know his grandfather, but then it occurred to me ... yes! He will know him. Bryce will know the beliefs and solid morals that his papa held through the man his dad is, and the example he sets for our children. So I hope that my children will grow up appreciating the simple things in life, taking pride in the things they've earned through hard work, and loving and appreciating family as their papa did."

After the services were over, Rob and I stayed briefly for the dinner our church had prepared for the family, said "thank you" to family and friends for coming, and then needed to cut our time short so we could go see how Bryce was doing. There was no time to grieve. I felt like we were just moving from one tragedy to another. My tears had dried up, and I was becoming concerned that something was wrong with me. *How could I not cry at my father-in-law's funeral?* I loved that man, and the sudden loss of his presence in our family was leaving a gaping wound. But I could not cry.

*Just keep moving. Just keep doing what needs done,* was all I could tell myself. Liza had volunteered to let Reyna stay the night with her so Rob and I could spend as much time as needed at the hospital with Bryce. We quickly ran home, switched our clothes, I pumped, and then we were off again.

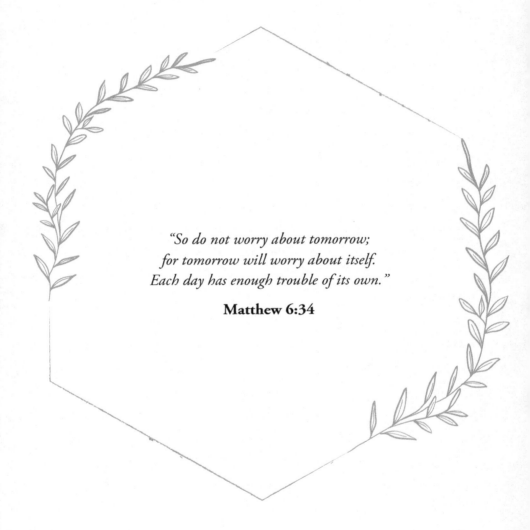

*"So do not worry about tomorrow;*
*for tomorrow will worry about itself.*
*Each day has enough trouble of its own."*

**Matthew 6:34**

# Sandbag Hats and Apologies

**W**hen we walked into Bryce's room, Rob and I noticed something on his head. "What in the world is on his head?" I asked. The nurse told us that Bryce kept fighting the anesthesia and would come out of sedation and start moving his head. Every time he did, the ventilator would move, and his heart rate would drop. "Infants metabolize and adjust quickly to the anesthetic, and we keep having to adjust the dose to keep Bryce sedated."

The sandbag hat was supposed to help make Bryce's head too heavy to move, but it wasn't really helping because each time it happened, I would have to hold my hand on the sandbag and hold Bryce's head still until they could get him the medicine. They were giving the anesthetic through the port in Bryce's thigh. The problem was that every time they needed to re-sedate him, the nurse would have to page someone with the key to the closet where the meds were, since it was a narcotic. This happened about every two hours and then about every hour. I stayed through the night, and Rob decided to go home. I think he needed to be at peace with the house to himself so he could finally grieve the loss of his dad.

Meanwhile, at the hospital, alarms were going off all night, and the nurse would yell, "He's bradying!"

I'd leap off of the sofa bed, put my hand on the sandbag hat and stand there with my hand on his head until they came running with the medicine for the port in Bryce's leg. Finally, when the doctors came for rounds at two in the morning, the tending doctor ordered the anesthetic to be given through a drip in Bryce's IV so they could stop running around trying to get it through his leg before he ripped the ventilator out—another three-hour night of sleep for me.

Sunday was relatively quiet, and Bryce remained on the ventilator. Now that he was receiving the anesthetic through the IV, he was resting more peacefully, and they no longer needed the sandbag hat. Rob had picked up Reyna from Liza's and brought her to the hospital. They would not let her back to see Bryce since it was flu season, but I wanted to see and spend time with her. I was worried about Reyna and what this had been doing to her. I knew she was still confused about losing her papa and was continuing to ask when he was coming home. I didn't want her worrying that Bryce and I were at the hospital and we wouldn't come home either.

While Rob was visiting Bryce, Reyna and I talked in the PICU waiting area. Reyna turned to me and said, "I'm sorry for making Bryce sick, Mommy."

If words could knock a person out of their chair, I was about to hit the floor. I was in shock! "What?" I asked.

She repeated it again, "I'm sorry for making Bryce have to come to the hospital."

I felt awful. Bryce had been in the hospital for four days now, and she had felt she was to blame this whole time. I hugged her and explained, "You did not cause this in any way, honey," I told her. "Bryce's heart got tired from working too hard and was having trouble beating. You did not do anything wrong."

I was so thankful she said what she had been feeling instead of keeping that self-guilt bottled inside. That night, when I talked to Rob later on the phone from the hospital, I told him what Reyna had said to me. "We have to watch our words from now on," I said. "We have been telling Reyna not to kiss Bryce on the face or touch his hands, especially when she comes home from daycare. Now she thinks she caused Bryce to get sick."

We were just trying to be careful, so Bryce didn't get the flu. I wish I had remembered that children take things so literally. Rob and I agreed that going forward, we would say, "Be sure to wash your hands so we keep everyone healthy."

⋄⬦⋄⬦⋄

After Rob had left for the night, the nurse told me, "We are going to start weening Bryce off the ventilator. We will start with a test first to see how he does when we turn off the machine and let him breathe on his own." She could tell this made me nervous. She reassured me, "The machine will be on 'auto,' so if Bryce doesn't breathe well on his own, it will be there as a backup."

I really wanted this to work because I was ready to take Bryce home so we could all be together as a family. The test went well, with backing the ventilator off. The nurses were pleased with how well Bryce's body handled the transition. On Monday, the next morning, they would talk to the doctors during rounds to see if we could proceed with removing the ventilator. Just as I started getting excited that we were making steps toward going home, Bryce's nurse said, "You will not be able to nurse him right away. He will have a feeding tube, but we will start giving him the breastmilk you have been stockpiling in the freezer. If Bryce tolerates the breastmilk and keeps it down, the feeding tube can come out."

*Dang it! Another day in the hospital! At least now I can hold him better, and there are not as many wires to manage.*

I went to the cafeteria for breakfast; then I went to pump. When I returned to the room, I noticed they had removed the ventilator. I could see Bryce's face better now, and he was starting to wake a little, though he was still on all the meds. Bryce had developed fluid in his lungs (common with patients on ventilators), so they were now giving him Lasix to flush the fluid out of his body.

*I can't take Bryce home with fluid in his lungs, or we'll be right back in here with pneumonia. Yet another obstacle to getting out of here.*

Monday afternoon, the chief of cardiac surgery stopped by to check on Bryce. I had not seen him since the day of Bryce's balloon valvuloplasty. "I am glad to see how well Bryce is doing. I am sorry he ended up in heart failure. You did everything we could have asked of you, and we didn't expect you to do what a nurse would do. We only asked you to be 'Mom,' and that is exactly what you did."

I appreciated him saying this and wondered if someone had told him I was blaming myself for not doing enough for Bryce. Then he began asking me questions about our trips to the pediatrician during the last two weeks. I told him, "I'm not pushing to get our pediatrician into trouble," though I was struggling internally because looking for someone to blame is human. I was angry with our pediatrician, and yes, I was looking for a new one, but I also knew he was not the only person I blamed.

Truth be told, I had my own guilt to deal with as I played over and over in my head what I could have done differently the last two weeks. I wished I had not accepted the pediatrician's prognosis and listened to my instincts that screamed something was wrong. Deep down, I wanted everything to be okay, and when I received the response I was hoping for, I didn't push past the fear to delve any further. I wished I had asked the pediatrician to call Bryce's heart doctor. I wished I had called the heart doctor.

The chief of cardiac surgery further explained, "I want you to know that the cardiac team and I are taking a hard look at Bryce's case to see where we went wrong. None of us anticipated that Bryce would take a turn for the worse as quickly as he did, and we want to learn from this so we don't have a repeat with another child."

I was grateful they were using Bryce's case as a learning experience because I would never want another family to experience what we just went through; however, I explained, "I am trying not to focus on the what-ifs or what might have been. I have my son, and I'm going to get to take him home soon. All I want to do now is focus on his future and being his mother."

As difficult as it is to share that I failed my infant son and nearly lost him because I didn't fight hard enough for him, I feel the need to share it, hoping it may help another family. If Bryce's story can teach others what to look for or what signs may be indicators that their infant is in heart failure, then our struggle, my failure, is not in vain.

Time for shift change again. I was beginning to dread it because shift change meant another nurse I had to get used to, and some had more empathy than others. I never knew which one I would get. I longed to hold Bryce free of wires, feed him when he was hungry, and take him home so his sister could get to know her little brother. I was hoping we would get a nurse who supports a breastfeeding mother. Never in my dreams did I think I would have to fight to nurse my child in a children's hospital. After all, their slogan was "Breast is best!" I was beginning to think that only applied when it doesn't interfere with measuring and chart tracking.

The new nurse was an older woman. She said, "I've worked in the PICU for seventeen years and predominantly as a cardiac nurse."

I was amazed that she had worked this floor for so many years, and I asked, "How have you lasted so long? I'm sure you have seen a lot of babies that don't have a positive outlook or ending."

"The good days outweigh the bad."

This encouraged me. *That says a lot about this hospital.*

The new nurse told me, "I am pushing for Bryce to come off the feeding tube so he can nurse. He was an established eater before he came in, and the best thing for him is to let him eat the way he knows how."

I liked this nurse … a lot.

Rob brought Reyna up to visit again. She wanted to go eat dinner in the little café at the hospital. She loved it there because they have little tables and chairs made just for kids, and she made us sit at them. Rob and I looked like giants in the chairs with our knees up to our chins while eating. We didn't stay too long at the café because I needed to pump again, and Rob had to work in the morning, which meant Reyna had to get up really early again to go to daycare. Her poor little eyes had dark black circles under them again from going to bed late and getting up early. I prayed that Bryce would be released the next day.

**I** got up Tuesday morning, pumped, and then raced down to the cafeteria to get back before rounds. When I returned to the room, I saw that the same nurse from the previous day was back. *Thank you, God!*

She said, "X-ray was here while you were gone. They want to see if the fluid in Bryce's lungs has changed. While they were taking x-rays, Bryce somehow managed to pull out his feeding tube. I was told to put it back in."

I was devastated because I did not want them shoving that tube up his tiny, fragile nose again. The last time I was there to see it, I had to listen to Bryce choking and sputtering as they forced it down his throat. I walked towards the bed, and the nurse was smiling at me. I looked at Bryce and back at her again. "What?"

"You didn't notice?"

I looked at Bryce again, and it hit me ... "The feeding tube is gone!" I exclaimed. "Are they coming back to place the tube later?"

She shook her head. "No."

"Does this mean I can feed him now?" I asked excitedly.

"Yep! When the doctors came by for rounds, I advocated that you should be allowed to feed him, and they agreed."

*Finally! I get to hold and nurse my baby free of tubes and wires.*

He still had the tiny oxygen nasal cannula, but that was only precautionary. Sure enough, I held my child in my arms, and he latched like we had never missed a beat. We were making progress toward home.

Later that day, another cardiologist stopped by to visit. I had not met him before, but I found out he was one of the many cardiologists working on Bryce's case. "I do the electrical work, whereas the cardiologist Bryce normally sees manages the plumbing. We are pleased with Bryce's charts and how well he is progressing." He sat and talked with me for a while. "When Bryce was admitted last Thursday, he only had 12 percent heart function."

I knew that Bryce's heart was in dire straits. I remembered seeing how it was barely beating on the screen the day of his last echo. *To hear it stated like this ... 12 percent function. How did Bryce last so long in that state? He had been in heart failure essentially for eight days before that and then had to hang on to life while his surgery was pushed from seven in the morning until three in the afternoon, a full twenty-four hours after he was admitted! God had us this whole time. God carried my son through this. I have no doubt. By the grace of God, my son is here.*

The cardiologist continued, "Bryce's heart had become dilated or enlarged. When the flaps became stuck together, Bryce's heart was working harder to push the blood through the tiny opening in the valve. After such a long time of trying to sustain that level of function, Bryce's heart got tired, and his left ventricle, what we like to refer to as the 'pumping chamber,' was tiring out. After the balloon cath procedure, Bryce now has 100 percent heart function. Bryce's heart is still dilated, and it will take some time to return to a normal size for a child his age. The leak that was created by the balloon cath is still somewhat of a concern, so we will continue to watch that."

They had been giving Bryce digoxin, a medicine that helps the heart maintain its rhythm and sustain function. The doctor mentioned, "You will go home with a prescription for digoxin, and Bryce will remain on it for a year, if not longer."

Then came the best part of the conversation ... "Bryce can go home!"

*I need to take him back to his normal cardiologist every two weeks, but we are out of here!*

I called Rob to tell him everything the doctor just explained and that Bryce had been released to go home. Rob said, "I will pick Reyna up after I get off work and come get you."

I responded, "No way! I am not waiting. My car is still here. I'm taking him home, and I'm picking Reyna up on my way!"

He tried to persist, but I was not about to give anyone an opportunity to change their mind. "We're leaving as soon as I can sign the papers," I told him.

Bryce left the hospital in style that day as they wheeled him to the parking deck in his car seat on a little red wagon. On our way home, I called Noah's Ark to tell them I'd like to stop to pick up Reyna and asked if they could get her ready so I wouldn't have to take Bryce into a room full of four-year-olds.

When I pulled up to the daycare, there was Miss Shauna, hand-in-hand with Reyna, standing there waiting for us. I didn't even have to get out of the car! *I absolutely love that woman. They are all so good to our family here.*

Reyna was thrilled to see her baby brother. She felt so proud because she got to sit beside Bryce in the car. Since he was in a rear-facing car seat, I asked her, "Could you help Mommy and keep an eye on him for me? Let me know if his head flops forward."

"I'm being asponsible," she said.

That night was the first night in a week that our whole family got to be home under one roof. I was both ecstatic and exhausted, but, above all, *thankful* to God that my son was saved and was in my arms again.

# PART TWO

# Finding Balance

*"Trust in the LORD with all your heart*
*And do not lean on your own understanding.*
*In all your ways acknowledge Him,*
*And He will make your paths straight."*

**Proverbs 3:5–6**

# 12

# Put On Your Own Mask

Nothing in this world measures up to rocking your baby to sleep. Holding that tiny bundle in your arms as you sway back and forth, cradling their soft head and admiring the beautiful miracle created from love. The sweet smell of baby lotion and lavender. It's a wonder that our carpets do not have paths worn in them from the many nights of cradling my babies while I walked them to sleep. "Walk and bounce. Walk and bounce," Rob used to call it. It was the only way I was successful in putting my babies to sleep.

Getting them to sleep was the easy part. *Keeping* them asleep when I'd lay them in their crib was a whole other adventure. Maybe it was because I never wanted to let them go, so I would clumsily place them in their bed, startling them awake as I bumped my head on the mobile. Now that we were home from the hospital, I was nervous about leaving Bryce sleeping alone in his crib. He felt so far away from me, especially after sleeping in his room for the past week and waking to every sound or noise he made.

I had ordered one of those baby monitors with a sensor underneath the mattress to detect if your baby stopped breathing. I needed peace of mind to sleep, and a close friend had suggested this monitor. I had to recondition my body to wake to a crying, hungry baby. It was definitely easier than waking to the alarm on my phone to pump, but it was still a transition to get used to all over again. When Bryce would cry in the night to eat, I would go to his room to feed him and walk him back to sleep. Then I would lay my hand on his chest, just to make sure he was breathing.

Before heading back to bed, I would seek God's grace and pray for my child, *Father in Heaven, King of the Universe, blessed are the innocent children. I come to You as a sinner, asking for forgiveness, for Your guidance to live life for You, and to thank You for Your Son, who died for our sins. Thank You for saving my child and granting us Your grace to give him a second chance at life. Father, I pray that You will place Your healing hands on my son and take this burden from him so that he may live a normal, healthy, and happy life. Please watch over him and bless him with the Son of Jesus Christ. Amen.*

I repeated this prayer every night as I watched my son sleep. Every night, I wished I could take his place and carry this burden for him. I would freely give up my own heart if it meant saving my child's life and if it afforded him the opportunity to live the life he deserved, free from pain and surgeries.

**M**y return-to-work date was fast approaching. I was nowhere near ready to go back, especially since I had received a promotion at the start of the year and had been made finance manager of the business I had been supporting. This time, I would be on my own without the safeguard of my previous manager. I would be directly reporting to the VP of Finance, which I was thrilled about when they gave me the news in January. Fast forward five weeks, and things have drastically changed. I now have an infant with a congenital heart condition who just had heart surgery a week ago, and my family is still mourning the loss of my father-in-law.

I called the nurse at work and explained everything that had happened in the last couple of weeks. "I'm concerned about coming back to work next week because Bryce is supposed to see his cardiologist every two weeks for the time being, and I can't take him to daycare and risk him getting sick."

The nurse recommended a counselor that might be able to help. "He may be able to recommend that you are placed on short-term sick leave."

I thanked her for her help and called for an appointment. I wasn't really sure what a counselor was going to do to help me, but if this was my chance to extend my maternity leave and be at home to care for my infant child, then I was going to try.

Preparing to leave the house the first day after being home from the hospital was a bit of a train wreck. I was up all night between feedings, making lists of everything I needed to do to prepare for the following day. My mom stayed with the kids while I went to my appointment. It was only scheduled for an hour, but I would be gone for three hours, including commute time, which meant I had to feed Bryce directly before I left and as soon as I got home. I prepared a bottle just in case Bryce got hungry earlier. Finally, it was time for me to head to the counselor's office.

The drive was long, and it was the first time I had been alone for this long in months. I didn't like being alone with my thoughts, so I played the radio as loud as I could stand it the entire way there. I arrived a few minutes early, so I walked inside and waited in the lobby. It was a small practice with two offices and a tiny kitchenette area. One of the office doors opened, and a tall man stepped out. He was friendly and soft-spoken. He motioned for me to step into his office, and I sat down. He introduced himself as Doug Pannette. I felt at ease as he asked me why I was there.

I began explaining about Bryce's birth and diagnosis and the roller coaster that ensued soon after. I didn't realize how difficult it would be to tell him how close I came to losing my baby. I broke down and started crying. I told him about my father-in-law being diagnosed with cancer the week after Bryce was born, then how he passed the same week Bryce went into heart failure. I was becoming inconsolable, and it was hard to breathe.

He handed me a box of Kleenex, offered me a glass of water, and told me to continue when I was ready. It was really the first time since everything had happened that I allowed myself to feel the pain of loss and the anguish of nearly losing my child. All the guilt I held in my heart came to the surface in one gigantic tidal wave. I spent the duration of the hour talking through tears about the heavy guilt I had been carrying—for working 70+ hours a week while pregnant, for not advocating hard enough for my child, and not doing more while he was in heart failure for over a week, for not being at home for my four-year-old daughter, for causing her to blame herself for her brother needing heart surgery. And most recently, guilt for needing to go back to work.

I explained that I was concerned about returning to work since I had recently been promoted to a higher-level role. "When I go back, I know I will be required to attend all the management meetings that my manager had previously attended. Now I will be expected to be at those meetings, in addition to maintaining all the previous reporting responsibilities." I was conflicted with how I would manage to keep focused at work on top of needing to take Bryce to heart appointments every other week.

Doug listened to me in earnest and then said, "You have been on autopilot these last couple of months and have not allowed yourself to feel. It's sort of a defense mechanism. Your body and mind just did what it needed to do to get through everything."

That day, talking to Doug was like someone had turned the water faucet on and let all those pent-up emotions out. I was diagnosed with post-traumatic stress disorder, postpartum depression, and acute stress. He provided a recommendation that I be placed on sick leave from work, and we set up monthly meetings moving forward to help me learn how to manage the things within my control. He used the analogy of what flight attendants tell people on airplanes. "We are of no use to anyone else until we take care of ourselves first. You need to learn to put on your own mask first. Only then will you be able to provide the full care that your children need, that your husband needs, and eventually what your work will need."

I cried the entire way home, and it felt great.

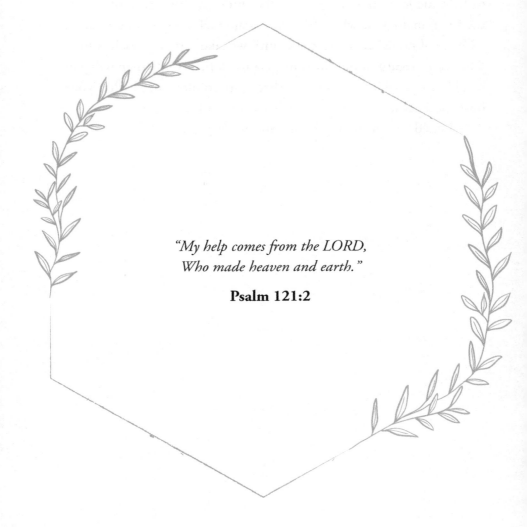

*"My help comes from the LORD,*
*Who made heaven and earth."*

**Psalm 121:2**

# 13

# One Little Lamb

The gradient of the blood flow had changed slightly since the balloon valvuloplasty surgery two weeks prior. The cardiologist was comfortable with Bryce's numbers, since they were still within the range he would like to see. I asked if there was anything I should be watching for, signs or symptoms to indicate an issue, and if so, what we should expect as next steps. This was the first time I was told about something called the "Ross Procedure."

The cardiologist explained, "My ultimate goal is to wait and let Bryce get older before we would have to do any other procedures. As long as Bryce continues to be so energetic, is eating well, and his pumping chamber continues to show that it is tolerating the amount of extra work it has to do to push the blood throughout his body, I would like to wait and continue to monitor him. We will continue to watch the leak that was created when they did the balloon cath. Right now, it is considered moderate. If it were to change and become severe, Bryce would need a valve replacement. I would not advise trying a valve repair. I would discuss with my team of cardiac doctors whether another balloon cath would be warranted or if they would move forward with a replacement. The goal being the least amount of risk and number of surgeries for Bryce. The last thing I would want is for Bryce to undergo valve repair, have it not work, and then subject him to a valve replacement. That would be two major surgeries for Bryce to recover from, which is a lot for his tiny body."

He continued, "If Bryce were to need a valve replacement at this young age, the heart surgeons would have to use his existing pulmonary valve and move it to replace his aortic valve. Then they would place a metal valve where Bryce's pulmonary valve had been. This is known as the 'Ross Procedure.' Using a metal valve would set Bryce up for multiple heart surgeries because the metal valve would not grow with him and would require replacement every one to two years. Right now, we do not have replacement aortic valves small enough for babies or toddlers. For adults, we can either use a cow, pig, or metal valve. The metal valves seem to be more durable and don't tire out. The cow or pig valve is similar to a human valve and could tire out. A metal valve would also mean that Bryce would be placed on blood thinners for the rest of his life."

Before leaving his office, the doctor told me, "We will continue to watch closely because Bryce's body is still adjusting to the new anatomy and needs to stabilize."

For Bryce's first checkup since the surgery, it was a fairly good report.

I drove home, trying to process everything the cardiologist had said, crying the whole way. It seemed I was crying more easily lately. I told this to my counselor, Doug, at our next session, and he said, "Everything is really raw right now. You need to allow yourself to grieve, forgive, and heal."

⬦⬦⬦⬦

Rob and I were discussing whether we should keep Bryce out of daycare, hire a nanny, or have me quit my job and stay home. The mounting medical bills arriving almost daily quickly cast the idea of me leaving my job out of the mix. Rob and I began weighing the pros and cons. We were familiar with the caregivers at the daycare since our daughter had been going there for the last four years. They had become like family to us, and the level of trust we would need to rebuild with a stay-at-home nanny was a high hill to climb, given Bryce's condition.

We considered asking Rob's mother to watch him as an option, but both agreed we didn't want to add anything to her plate as she was still grieving the loss of her husband. I had talked to the cardiologist during our last appointment and asked his opinion about placing Bryce in daycare, and he said, "You need to do what your family needs to do. If that means daycare, we will manage through it."

Eventually, Rob and I mutually agreed that daycare was the best place for Bryce. Knowing that having a child in daycare also comes with the many germs that kids spread in such a close environment, I reminded Rob that the teachers at the daycare have to take CPR classes so they would be trained in the event of an emergency. We agreed that it was also best for Reyna to have some stability since she had practically grown up with the kids there, as well as the caregivers. It was settled. I called our daycare to get Bryce on the schedule to begin attending in July, when I was expected to return to work.

With my return-to-work date only a month away, the sessions with my counselor turned to working on building skills to limit stress. I was concerned about having to retell my story over and over to friends at work. After the waterworks that first day trying to tell Doug my story, I feared what would happen when my co-workers began asking me about the baby or asking why I extended my leave longer than expected. Obviously, I knew I did not have to share any personal health information because of protection by the HIPPA laws, but my concern was how to tell my friends and close co-workers who had a genuine concern for me and my family.

I told Doug I wanted to avoid spending my workday answering questions and catching people up on what happened. We began strategizing on the best way I should handle this. First, I decided to go back to work part-time to start. This would allow me to ease into things and see how it went. It would also send a signal to co-workers that I was not quite ready to jump in with both feet … I was merely sticking my toe in the water.

Our second strategy was for me to devise a list of close co-workers with whom I felt okay with sharing our story. Then I would write an email summarizing the events I was comfortable sharing and send it to the co-workers on my list. This would allow me to get in front of most of the questions people may have wanted to ask when they saw me in the hallway or stopped by my office. I also updated Doug on the latest visit with cardiology. The ten-week post-op appointment was the first time I had heard the cardiologist use the word "stable" in reference to Bryce's heart, showing that it was recovering well. They were still monitoring the leak in his valve and the gradient to make sure it didn't become restricted as he grew.

At our last visit, I also found out that Bryce's heart had shrunk back to a normal size for his age. The dilation that had occurred when he was in heart failure was gone. I could finally breathe a sigh of relief that things were moving in the right direction, and Bryce's progress was all very positive.

**O**n the first day back at work, I was admittedly a bit of an emotional train wreck. I was still feeling very conflicted about going back to work and leaving Bryce at daycare. I had not really slept much the night before. Between feeding the baby, worrying that I would forget to take my breast pump to work, or not taking enough bottles for Bryce to daycare, my mind could not stop stressing about all the things I was probably behind on at work. When I walked to the kitchen that morning, I reached for Bryce's bottles to begin filling them with the liquid gold I had been stockpiling in our freezer for months. Just before I started to pour, I looked down at my hands and realized I had the coffee pot and was about to pour coffee into the baby's bottle. *Get it together, Tracy! This is going to be a long day!*

We pulled into the daycare, and Reyna was excited to show her teachers her new baby brother. She asked, "Can I walk Bryce to the Lamb Room?" All the rooms at the Noah's Ark daycare were named after animals, and the infant room was the Lamb Room.

Reyna skipped beside me as we walked to Bryce's room. She helped hand Bryce's bottles to the teacher as I unloaded the diapers and baby wipes in his bin. I noticed there were no other babies in the room yet. "Am I dropping off really early, or are the other babies coming later in the day?"

"Bryce is the only baby on the schedule."

I was shocked (and thrilled) to hear this. "Seriously?" I asked.

She reached for Bryce as I handed him to her. "Yep. It's just you and me today, buddy."

I drove to work so happy and relieved that Bryce would have the sole attention of his caregiver, and I wouldn't have to worry about any other babies who may be sick or spreading germs. It would turn out that Bryce remained the only baby in the Lamb Room that entire summer. Never in all the years that I had taken my daughter to daycare had I ever seen only one single baby in the Lamb Room. God's grace had been bestowed upon us yet again.

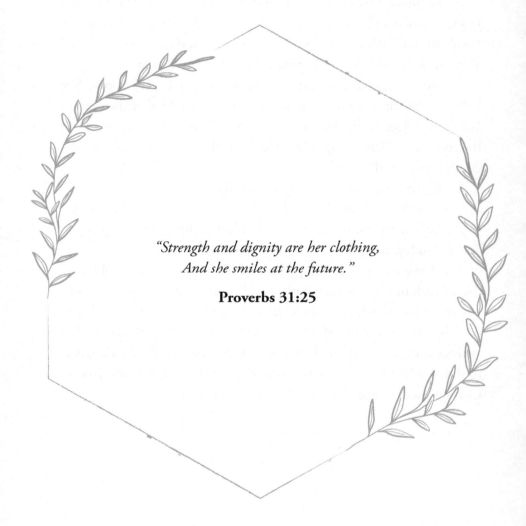

*"Strength and dignity are her clothing,*
*And she smiles at the future."*

**Proverbs 31:25**

# 14

# It's Okay to Ask for Help

At the first team business meeting I attended upon returning to work full-time, I felt like the new kid at school. While I was out, so many new people were hired that I could barely keep up with all the new names. The general manager (GM) had hired a new business development director, a new research & development director, two new marketing managers, a product manager, and a new administrative assistant.

With all the new business leaders in the group, I was overwhelmed with requests for new reports or reports specific to their market or region. I started finding myself with countless meetings consuming my days, which led me to logging onto my computer to get my "actual" work done after I put the kids to bed at night. I did not have a finance analyst like the other business finance managers because it was a new business group and was considered a smaller business than the other existing businesses. Without an analyst to help me with the reporting requirements, my days and nights were monopolized by work, and I was spending less and less time with my kids.

I felt like the only quality time I had with my baby was on the days he had an appointment to see the cardiologist. Even appointment days were not safe from the clutches of my demanding job. Taking time off for a doctor's appointment, especially one that was not for me, felt like I was being derelict in my duties. As the only female business finance manager, I was the only one taking off work to take my kids to doctors' appointments. All the other male finance managers either had wives that didn't work or their wives were the primary person to take their kids to appointments. I did not want the stigma that I was not pulling my weight or working any less than my male counterparts, so I would log onto the computer and make up the time I had missed due to taking Bryce to his appointments.

It didn't matter that I had already been working 60-hour work weeks. A manager once told me that perception is reality, and I was not about to allow anyone's perception of me to be that I was a slacker. I later found out through talking with my female colleagues that they also felt this way and often did the same as me—made up the hours they were off taking kids to appointments.

Some men in our office would take an afternoon off to go play golf together. I was invited to go a couple of times, and that was when I realized I had been placing this false stigma on myself. None of the men in my office considered me a slacker. No one ever even hinted at this notion, but it was a guilt, a burden that I had inflicted on myself. On the golf course, I also learned from my male counterparts that "it's okay to say no" to some of the requests I had been getting. They encouraged me, "Sometimes asking more questions to find out what they really need can save time spending hours on something that wasn't needed."

During one of my monthly sessions with Doug, we discussed my need to overcompensate to avoid being perceived as less than hard-working. I also told him I didn't know how much longer I could sustain working 60- and 70-hour workweeks, trying to nurse and care for an infant. He encouraged me to ask for help. Through talking to Doug, I realized that, though the business I supported was smaller in terms of earnings, the time and effort it took to put slides together was the same as all the other finance managers, who all had an analyst to support them. With our group's growing number of business leaders, the demands for new reports had increased exponentially.

I agreed to talk to my manager to see how we could improve the situation. I scheduled a meeting with the VP of Finance, who was now my boss, and laid out my case for a new headcount to help support me. He agreed, "It is probably time to add the resource," and then reminded me, "It will probably take a couple of months to get someone hired and trained." He encouraged me to ask for help earlier and not to wait until I had my head under water before raising my hand.

We also talked about my work-life balance, and he explained he expects his direct reports to be professionals. "We know better than anyone else what is on our plates," he continued. "Some months, we may be required to work over and put in extra time, and other months we may be slower. It should all balance out. I expect each of my direct reports to manage their own time."

After hearing this, I no longer made up my time when I took my kids to an appointment if I had already put in extra hours. I also stopped trying to overcompensate for a stigma that wasn't there.

⋄⋌⋋⋌⋋⋄

During Bryce's six-month wellness visit in July, his new pediatrician informed me, "Due to Bryce being in a daycare setting, the heart doctor and I recommend that Bryce receive Synagis shots."

Synagis is a series of virus-blocking antibodies that prevent babies from getting RSV (respiratory syncytial virus). He said, "A hundred percent of kids under the age of two will develop RSV in a daycare setting, and this could be detrimental for a child with a congenital heart disease." Then the shocking part of the conversation: "Each shot costs approximately $2,000, and Bryce will need one shot per month during RSV season, November through March."

Yes, you read that correctly—$2,000 per shot for five months!

He continued, "The insurance company will likely deny him, so we need to file for it now so we have time to appeal before he needs the first shot."

After several calls to the pediatrician and help from a nurse at the pediatrician's office who made calls on our behalf, we finally got the visiting nurse scheduled for Bryce's first Synagis shot on November 15th, 2013. On the day the nurse was scheduled to visit, the medicine was shipped to my house, and a notification was sent to the nurse confirming its delivery. I promptly placed the medicine in the refrigerator, awaiting his arrival. The nurse would then weigh Bryce to determine how much medicine he needed.

The December visit did not go as smoothly as the one in November. First of all, when I opened the door, and Bryce saw the male nurse standing there, he remembered him from the last month and turned to run and hide. Much to my chagrin, after convincing Bryce to come back so the nurse could weigh him, the nurse said, "He has grown since November, which requires a higher dose. I will have to split it between two shots in each leg."

*I may need to sit down to open that bill when we get it ... two shots at $2,000 in one sitting? Just how much will this bill be when we get to March?*

We were still working with the insurance company, and the nurse in our pediatrician's office had managed to obtain a coupon for us to help offset the cost. I never knew there was such a thing as a vendor coupon for prescriptions, but I was happy one existed and even more thankful the nurse helped us get it.

⋯⋯⋯

According to Doug, with Bryce's birthday approaching and the impending anniversary of his balloon heart cath, I was struggling with suppressed anxiety. Every time I would see an appointment reminder pop up, it was a giant slap in the face of reality. To make matters worse, I had a work conflict with Bryce's next appointment. Doug reminded me, "You are working toward getting better at asking people for help, so accepting Rob on his offer to take Bryce is a step in the right direction. It may also be helpful for you to connect with groups in the area for parents with congenital conditions. The hospital may be able to put you in touch with groups, and it would be good for you to find support from parents who have already gone through this."

Following his recommendation, I discovered several Facebook groups for Heart Moms, one for kids who have had the Ross Procedure, a group for children with bicuspid aortic valves, and so many more. At first, I found it extremely overwhelming because I read through countless stories shared by parents of children born with various heart issues. Many stories were encouraging and gave me hope. Then there were the posts of moms mourning the loss of their heart babies.

One night, I lay awake, captivated by the endless stream of stories, and I could not pry my eyes away from my phone as I lay there crying, my heart breaking for the mothers who had to figure out how to live life after losing their child. It bore a hole in my soul and placed such a profound weight on my heart; I had to stay off Facebook for weeks to shake the fear it caused in me. When I recalled the experience to Doug, he recommended, "Try to use the sites to gain knowledge to prepare yourself. The better we can prepare ourselves for what to expect next, the better equipped you are to handle it when the time arrives."

I began sharing my story in the groups. I found this helped me feel like I was returning some of the blessings we had received by giving other parents a window into what they might expect. I also was able to connect with several moms whose story was very similar to ours. These moms became friends to lean on when the anxiety from appointment reminders put me right back into a hospital room with my baby attached to countless wires. They became a voice of encouragement when illness found its way into my home and filled me with worry. A whole world of support and opportunities to learn from one another was opened for me when I made the effort to research and find other families going through very similar challenges. The greatest gift I knew how to give another mom going through something similar was to share, listen, and let her know that someone else understood the pain and worry she was going through. That is also what I hope to achieve with this book.

The snow was really coming down, making it difficult to distinguish the lines on the side of the road from the snow. I had to leave extremely early to make the long commute to downtown Cleveland on the snow-covered roads. It was January 2014, and time for another global business meeting. This time I was not in labor and expecting a baby, but my baby was scheduled for his heart checkup today, and I was going to miss it. It was the first one I had missed since he was born a year ago. This was the price I had to pay for being a working mom. I knew he was in good hands, and I was glad that Rob was there to talk with the heart doctor, but it didn't make me feel any less guilty for not being there to hear what he had to say firsthand.

I was scheduled to be one of the first presenters in the morning, and I was able to get through my slides without an issue. I had such a hard time staying focused during the remainder of the meeting because my heart and mind were wondering how Bryce's appointment was going. During the morning session, we had a presenter from the Cleveland Clinic speak to our team. They were discussing success stories they had been a part of, helping heart patients with valve replacements, specifically advancements in catheterizations. The presenter explained, "Our work contributed to the success rates due to the invention of a guard that is placed on the catheter as a lead. This guard stopped the catheter from piercing the artery as it is guided through the heart."

He also provided statistics on how many patients were lost before the guard was made available. If I had been listening to this presentation on any other day, I probably could have appreciated the blessing of the advancement that helped save so many lives of people who undergo a heart cath. On this day, it was too much to bear. I had to get up and leave the room. I went to the restroom and cried.

Two of my friends followed me to ensure I was okay. They stayed with me until I was ready to go back to the meeting. While we were waiting for the next break, Rob called with an update on Bryce's check-up. He said, "Bryce's numbers haven't changed, and the leak didn't get bigger. His next appointment is in three months."

I felt a wave of relief wash over me, knowing Bryce was still doing well and that I did not have to do it all. Rob did just fine taking Bryce to his appointment. Deep down, I knew he would.

Learning to ask for help was becoming an easier thing for me to do, and I was beginning to understand it is a pathway to healing.

*"Treat people the same way you want them to treat you."*

**Luke 6:31**

# 15

# Setting Healthy Boundaries

The soft purr of the engine could be heard starting up in the distance as I stretched my arm to extend the reach of the remote start. My car sat alone in the parking lot about a thousand feet away. *This is starting to get old.* I was among the few people who used the 8:30 to 5:30 flex schedule since I had small children to get up in the morning and I had an hour commute. Since I was one of the last to arrive in the mornings, I was typically parked the farthest away from the door. I couldn't remember the last time I was able to leave at 5:30, though.

Our new business development director had made a habit of stopping by my office on his way out at 5:00 p.m. with a list of demands he needed by 8:00 the next morning. While he was sitting at home with his family, I was stuck in the office plugging away at his last-minute requests until 8:30 at night. I called Rob to see if I could talk to the kids before they went to bed.

"What is going on, Tracy? This is the third time in two weeks."

"I know. I'm sorry. Can I please talk to Reyna before she goes to bed?"

"She's in the bathtub. Was it that same guy demanding stuff again? Did you tell him 'no' this time?"

I told Rob, "I'm leaving now. I'll see you in an hour. Please try to keep the kids up just a little longer so I can kiss them goodnight."

This had been a recurring event lately, and the worst part was that it was starting to trickle down to the other managers. They would see my light was still on in my office, so they would swing by and either start chatting with me or give me an, "Oh, by the way, if you have time…." They all knew I was online at night when I signed onto my laptop after I had put the kids to bed, and they had started sending me instant messages asking me questions at one in the morning. Clearly, if I was online that late at night, it was not because I had nothing better to do.

Monopolization of my time had also become an area I was fighting to reign in. During the budget season in the early fall of 2013, a marketing manager scheduled a meeting to walk through the resource needs for the next year. The meeting was adjacent to a personal appointment I had on my calendar. The meeting was being held in my office, and it ran over. I had placed the time on my calendar as a way to block out personal time for me to use the breast pump. As the meeting ran later, I was becoming uncomfortable, and I was struggling with how to excuse myself without telling him my personal business. I finally stood up and said, "I need to use the restroom."

That prompted him to look at his watch. "Oh, I guess we ran a little over."

*Yeah, by an hour!* I was in pain and irritated—with him for being disrespectful of my time and with myself for allowing it. This same scenario had played out multiple times while I was trying to continue breastfeeding and ultimately became part of the reason my milk was drying up. I scheduled these "personal meetings" to coincide with when I would normally feed the baby if I was at home. Each time I missed pumping was signaling my body that the baby didn't need to eat, which meant my body didn't need to produce the milk during that time.

Our company's only lactation room was clear across campus at the infirmary, and it took ten minutes to walk there from my office. I had submitted a work order to have maintenance install window blinds in my office so I could just lock my office door and pump there to save time walking back and forth. Even so, I found I was able to pump less and less. When I returned from the restroom, and the marketing manager had left, I locked my door and turned off the light. Turning my office light off served two purposes: first, it helped to calm me and put me in a quiet, peaceful environment, and second, it made others think I was out of the office so they wouldn't try to interrupt me, with the exception of one time when someone knocked on the door. My light was off, and I had already started to pump when I heard the knock. A rush of panic overcame me as I tried to recall if I had locked the door. Then I heard the doorknob twist as if someone were trying to open the door. Thank goodness it was locked, and they left!

I raised the issue with Doug, my counselor, regarding the stress I was feeling from simply trying to maintain being able to nurse my baby and the guilt I felt for allowing others to take that away from me. We discussed ideas for managing these situations when they arose and practiced the techniques I had planned to implement through roleplay. Doug would play the part of someone trying to hold a meeting with me, and it was my job to find ways to set the boundaries. For one example, I suggested, "I could tell the person requesting the meeting that I have another meeting directly following."

Doug encouraged me, "That is a great way to tell people you have a hard stop and puts them on notice that you cannot run over."

"If I am responding to a meeting invite, I could send a response with my acceptance stating that I have another commitment directly after. If more time is needed, we can reschedule for another day and time."

The last bit of advice Doug suggested was to tell me, "Stop feeling obligated to accept meeting invites if they conflict with your schedule." This sounded like common sense, I know, but this was something I needed to remind myself, that sometimes my life and family needed to be a priority too, and it is okay to propose an alternate day or time.

The last straw for me came when Bryce came down with an intestinal virus after he was already fighting double ear infections. It was his ninth ear infection in seven months. Rob and I had been up with Bryce every two hours and had to change his clothes and the bedding every time. Rob stayed home with Bryce the next day because I had meetings at work. I stayed home with him on the third day. Bryce was still not feeling well, but at least had stopped vomiting. I was becoming concerned that Bryce may be dehydrated, so I took him to see the pediatrician.

By the time we made it to the doctor's office, I had noticed that Bryce no longer had tears when he cried. I was also worried that he couldn't keep his antibiotics down, so his ear infections would not heal. The pediatrician sent me to the emergency room (ER) after examining Bryce. He ended up being admitted for severe dehydration, and they wanted to monitor him because of his heart condition. They had placed an IV in his tiny arm and covered it with a hard plastic cover so he wouldn't pull it out. Then they covered it with a sock. Thankfully, his antibiotics could be administered through the IV too.

Although they had the plastic cover pretty well secured, I still had to keep an eye on him because he would bang the plastic sock on the bed, get the IV tangled, and try to rip it out. I stayed in the hospital with him that night and had my work phone with me. I was trying to answer anything urgent and let people at work know I did

SETTING HEALTHY BOUNDARIES

not have my laptop with me. Bryce ended up being released two days later on a Sunday afternoon.

Sunday morning, I received an email from one of the marketing managers with a request. He ended his email, "Your prompt response is expected."

It was a Sunday, so it wasn't even a regular workday. I tried to remember everything I had discussed with Doug about setting healthy boundaries. I responded to the marketing manager, "I am currently in the hospital with my son, and I will not be able to provide you with a response today." I further explained, "In the future, I will need twenty-four hours' notice, at a minimum, for any requests. If something requires an in-depth analysis, my turnaround time will be adjusted accordingly. Thank you for your understanding."

I was beginning to build up those personal boundaries and set realistic expectations. It was time that I demanded the same respect I provided to others. I also began turning off my instant message program when I logged on at night so that my active status was not visible to those tempted to send me requests in the middle of the night, simply because they saw my green light was on.

◇◇◇◇◇

In an attempt to gain more efficiency, I contacted a co-worker with a reputation for being very skilled in consolidating reports. He and I spent two hours combing through the list of reports I had been managing separately, and he provided some helpful tips to consolidate. It took some time and effort to finalize, but I successfully consolidated all the market segments, regional, global, and regional-by-market-segment reporting, into one report. I rolled the new report out during a monthly team business meeting and walked everyone through how to use the drop-down boxes. The team seemed on board with the new reports, which saved me hours of time.

When I published the new report and sent it to the team the next month, the new business development director appeared in my office doorway. "Thanks for sending the reports," he said. "Could you just take a screen print of my segment and put it into an email, and send it to me monthly?"

I responded, "I would be happy to show you how to navigate the report to filter on your segment." I stood up and said, "I can show you how to get to your data to print it. Do you want to go to your office and pull it up so I can walk you through it?"

"No, that's okay. I don't want to have to open the file. I like the format of the file you sent. It would just be easier for me if you could send me my results in a print screen monthly."

"I created the report to help save me some time because it is becoming extremely inefficient with so many reports and everyone needing a different report. I would prefer that the end users filter the report to what they need and then save the file with your filters or print it, but I will not have time to send you print screens every month."

He went to the GM to complain about me. The GM pulled me into his office and said, "I was told you refused to provide the team with the reports they need."

I explained, "I am not the business development manager's personal clerk, and I have twelve other managers who also need reports, which is why I created the consolidated reporting. My suggestion would be to ask the business admin to help send him the print screens. She is good at Excel and could help him, but I will not have time to do that every month."

It was becoming apparent that the team that had grown used to taking advantage of me would not be very accepting of my pushing back. Although I was learning to set clear boundaries, they were unwilling to change their behavior, and I was unwilling to return to that unhealthy working style. So I talked to my manager about it, and he fully supported me in setting boundaries and demanding mutual respect from my team. He told me, "You are their peer, not their direct report, and while there may be some cases when something comes up at the last minute, not everything should be a fire drill."

After hearing about the Sunday incident, he also agreed. "They need to manage their requests to afford you ample time to respond, and no one should be demanding a response from you on a Sunday."

All of this sounded encouraging to me; however, as time passed, it became apparent that changing the team's behavior would be more challenging than expected.

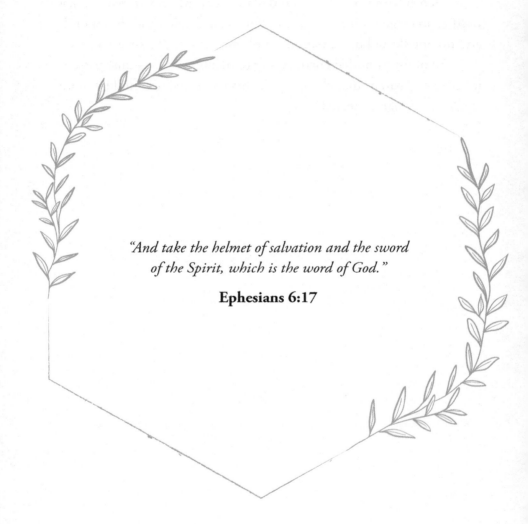

*"And take the helmet of salvation and the sword of the Spirit, which is the word of God."*

**Ephesians 6:17**

# 16

# Focus on What You Can Control

"**D**on't tap on the glass, honey," I said to Bryce as he eagerly watched for the Nemo fish to swim back around. We were back in the pediatrician's office; I suspected another ear infection. This would be the tenth time in eight months. Each time, they seemed to give us a more potent antibiotic, and I was becoming concerned that Bryce's body would stop reacting to the antibiotics, which would not be good if he came down with something more serious than an ear infection.

Finally, a woman walked into the lobby and called out, "Bryce."

The doctor inspected Bryce's ears. "Double ear infection," as suspected. "We need to give Bryce Rocephin, an antibiotic. It needs to be administered in the office because it is an injection. Bryce will need one shot in each leg for the next three days."

"This poor kid. He is due for his next RSV shot in four days. Eight shots in four days is a lot for such a little kid."

She reassured me, "The antibiotics won't interfere with the Synagis shots, and getting the antibiotics into Bryce's system this way will help fight the infection more aggressively."

Since he had basically just finished the last antibiotics two weeks prior, and the Azithromycin clearly was not strong enough to knock out the bacteria, they wanted to try this route. He had already taken Amoxicillin for the ear infection he had two months prior in December, so he had graduated to injections of antibiotics.

The nurse entered the room, and Bryce was not taking his eyes off her. As soon as she wiped his leg with the alcohol to clean it, Bryce started screaming. I was doing my best to calm him while she finished the second one. He had received RSV shots for the last three months, so he knew the drill. The nurse was quick, and once she finished, I scooped Bryce up in my arms and gave him hugs and kisses. I told him, "It's over, buddy. We're going home now."

I left the office with a referral letter for the ear, nose, and throat (ENT) doctor and two appointments to see the tech for the following two days for the remainder of the antibiotic shots. Thankfully, Rob would be taking Bryce for the next two days. I hate always feeling like I was the bad guy because I usually was the one taking him for shots. Rob would share in the agony this time.

*Poor Bryce. He doesn't get a break from any of it,* I thought on the drive home.

❖❖❖❖

The next month, March 2014, Bryce had his surgery for the ear tubes. The tubes would help his ears drain properly to avoid bacteria collecting in the eardrum and turning into ear infections. I had also taken Bryce to a urologist to see if they would also do his circumcision while he was under anesthesia. I know this sounds horrible; let me explain. When Bryce was born, the cardiologist would not let the obstetrician perform the circumcision because he was worried it would overwork Bryce's heart. Now that Bryce was fourteen months old and his heart was stable, the cardiologist signed off to allow us to have it done in parallel with the ear tubes. When

I went to see the urologist, I was unexpectedly met with obstinance about why I wanted to have Bryce circumcised and given a lecture on how the trend he was seeing lately was that people were not doing that anymore.

We had promised my father-in-law when he was in the hospital that we would see that Bryce was circumcised. He was adamant that he didn't want Bryce to endure that pain as an adult, and I was resolved to keep our promise to Bill. I was no longer the mom who sat quietly and accepted everything a doctor told me without considering my own thoughts and knowledge. I learned my lesson about not going with what I know feels right. "I am not here because of some religious purpose," I sternly said. "My son has already been through a lot. Do you honestly think I would be sitting in your office if I didn't have a strong reason for wanting this done? I have a family member who had to have a circumcision at forty years old because the hole grew shut, and I am not about to let my son go through the pain that man endured. "

The urologist agreed, so there we were with poor Bryce, sore at both ends. They gave Bryce a nerve block to help with pain management for twenty-four hours post-surgery. Pain block or not, his circumcision looked awful. He had eight stitches and glue on the surgery site, so I had to keep it covered with A&D ointment so it wouldn't stick to his diaper. He slept most of the day once we were home from surgery, only woke to eat, and then fell back asleep. Only when he wet his diaper did he wake up crying until I could get him cleaned and changed.

When Rob came home from work, he changed Bryce and saw how purple and swollen he was; he exclaimed, "Oh, wow! We should not have done this!"

My head snapped around, and I spat back, "Hey! Don't say that! I'm the one that had to take him for the surgery. Besides, we agreed we did this to avoid him going through what your dad went through."

As the year pressed on, work was beginning our busy season, typically starting in July with strategic planning and moving directly to budget season for the duration of the year. I was beginning to struggle internally with a constant push-pull between my work and family responsibilities. I felt a constant tug that I was not living the life God had planned for me. I prayed God would show me the path to follow. I prayed without ceasing, as it says in 1 Thessalonians 5:16–18:

> "Rejoice always, pray without ceasing, in everything give thanks; for this is the will of God for you in Christ Jesus."

**S**ometime around Thanksgiving 2014, I was in a meeting with my manager. He mentioned a role may be opening up in operations. I had not told him I had updated my resume and was already interviewing externally. I was shocked and thrilled to hear more about the role. It sounded like something perfect for me. My manager asked if I had any plant experience, and I said, "Yes, I worked at a plant for ten years before coming here."

He gave me the hiring manager's name and said to reach out if I was interested. I shared with my manager that I had been going to counseling. I don't know why I never felt comfortable telling him before. I suppose it was fear of any negative connotations with someone needing counseling. I didn't want him to think I was unstable. I explained I was seeing a counselor who specialized in stress management, and he was really helping me set healthy boundaries and limit my focus to things within my control.

He responded, "I could see a difference in you. I thought you were getting more comfortable in the role and building the confidence to push back."

"I definitely think it is both. I could not have done one without the other."

One particular instance occurred between the GM and me, which became the turning point when I realized I was finally setting healthy boundaries and focusing on the things I could control. The strategy review was quickly approaching, and the team was behind in finalizing our slides. The GM had told my manager, "Clear guidelines were not set for the team." The GM felt it was my fault the team was behind in getting slides ready to share with the Segment VP.

When my manager questioned me about it, I pulled up the strategy presentation that had been shared at the kickoff meeting in which the timeline, with deadlines, was communicated to all commercial leaders. I also shared the Excel template I provided for each region for their strategy roll-up. Every Excel tab, for each region and market segment, had the words, "Final submission due to Tracy Ripley on 7/31/2014." at the top of every tab within the Excel file.

After a conversation with my manager, the GM came to my office and stood in the doorway. He began shouting at me. I started to raise my voice to match his. Then I remembered the lessons I had learned. I recognized that my heart was racing. This was that fight-or-flight thing Doug talked about. With the GM standing in the doorway, I couldn't get up to leave. I certainly didn't want to give him an opportunity to say I shoved past him. I slowed my breathing. I lowered my voice to a calm tone and then said, "I think we should discuss this at another time, when we've both had a chance to calm down. This conversation isn't going anywhere, and if we continue, I feel it will lead to both of us saying things we will regret."

Immediately, the GM was visibly angry, turned around, slammed the door, and left. This was not the last time I would find myself in a contentious disagreement with the GM, but it was the first time I realized that because I recognized and controlled my emotions, I was able to defuse the situation from escalating into a shouting match and avoided allowing someone else's emotions to dictate my actions.

# PART THREE

## Letting Go

*"But I say to you who hear, love your enemies,*
*do good to those who hate you,*
*bless those who curse you, pray for those who are abusive to you."*

**Luke 6:27–28**

# Most People Have
# Good Intentions

As I rinsed the soap from Bryce's hair, I noticed something blue in his right ear. It was just inside the ear canal, but so tiny I didn't want to risk shoving it further in his ear. I asked Bryce, "Did you shove playdough in your ear at school again today?"

"No."

I yelled for Rob. "Please, come upstairs and bring your flashlight."

While Rob was getting his flashlight, Bryce dried off, and I helped him get dressed. Rob used his tweezers to pull the blue thing out … it was Bryce's ear tube.

"Darn it! It's flu season! He's going to start having ear infections all over again," I sighed.

I was grateful that I had been in my new role for seven months because I knew another surgery was imminent. I accepted the role in operations that my previous manager had mentioned to me and transitioned in April 2015. For the first time in over two years, I enjoyed going to work again. I had ten direct reports that were outstanding and easy to get along with, and the best part was that my new manager was the same one I had when I was pregnant with Bryce. He had also moved to operations and was my new boss. It was great because I didn't have to go through the whole backstory of Bryce's history or explain why I needed to take vacation for his heart appointments. I was finally beginning to have the work-life balance I needed. As expected, another round of ear infections soon began, and we were once again fighting a constant battle with stronger antibiotics each round.

**M**om and I were in the waiting room with Bryce. He seemed a bit scared this time and clingy with me. It only took three months, and we were back in March 2016 to have a second set of tubes put in. The ENT felt it was necessary to take Bryce's adenoids out as well because they were enlarged and blocking the drainage from his ears. The nurse called us back and asked me, "Would you help him get changed into the hospital pajamas?"

When I went to sit Bryce on the bed, he clung to me, crying, "No, Mama! No!"

*He must remember being here last year when he had surgery to open the tear duct in his eye.* We tried to let his eye go as long as we could, hoping it would correct itself, but the pediatrician referred us to an ophthalmologist when Bryce turned two because it was still clogged. I gave Bryce his Simba blanket and told him, "I'm not leaving. We need to get your clothes changed."

He reluctantly let me leave his side while I searched the cupboard to find pajamas to fit him. Once he was changed, the nurse asked Bryce, "Do you want to go for a walk?" They wanted to see how he would do with being separated from me.

He reached for my hand and said, "Come on, Mama." This wasn't going to be as easy as the last two procedures. He was becoming much more aware and familiar with this place.

The nurse asked me, "Do you want me to give him something to calm his nerves?"

"Is it okay to take with his heart condition?"

"Yes, it is. It will make him forget the entire procedure. He will only remember being with you and waking up," she assured me.

So I agreed. Soon they came for him again, and Bryce walked away holding the nurse's hand, with his Simba blanket in the other. When they came to get us to see him in recovery, Bryce was crying, and his voice was hoarse. He let my mom and me take turns holding him as he woke from anesthesia. When the nurse offered him a popsicle, he sat straight up. Popsicles were the way to this three-year-old's heart.

In preparation for Bryce's upcoming surgery for the second set of ear tubes, I tried to remember everything I had been working toward, focusing on the things I could control. I reached out to my friends on social media to vent and find support. For the most part, I received words of encouragement and love. I should always remember that when I asked for comments on social media, I was going to get the good with the bad. That was a hard lesson for me to learn. A couple of people commented that tubes are an "easy fix" and a "quick surgery," and they are correct in those statements.

However, I felt they were insensitive, given that this was now Bryce's fourth surgery in three years. Any parent who has ever had to hand their child over to medical staff for surgery knows that it is always a big deal, no matter how quick the surgery is. This would be the fourth time I handed my child to a surgeon who I've only had a handful of conversations with, an anesthesiologist I've had a three-minute conversation with, and a couple of operating room nurses who I would probably not see or speak to and I was expected to trust them with one of my most precious treasures on this earth.

These types of responses from people were becoming increasingly bothersome to me and became a point of focus during my stress management sessions with my counselor, Doug.

I needed to work toward ignoring unsolicited advice and realizing that it can be difficult for people to truly understand what I was going through. Often, it is hard for a person to relate to what someone else is going through if they have never been in their shoes. When people would ask if Bryce was doing better, they wanted to hear that he was cured. Don't get me wrong, I wanted that for Bryce too, but I knew this was not like the flu or a broken bone that would heal in six to eight weeks. This would be a lifelong journey for Bryce. The next popular question I usually got from people was, "Is this his last surgery?"

My answer was always the same: "We know he will need more surgeries in the future, but no one knows how many or when. Even the doctors are only giving their best guesses. Only God knows the plan for Bryce." As Jeremiah 29:11 tells us:

> "For I know the plans that I have for you," declares the Lord, "plans for prosperity and not for disaster, to give you a future and a hope."

A conversation with a work friend had me particularly bothered by their seemingly insensitive comments. The person had asked me about the next steps for Bryce. When I finished explaining what I had been told about the Ross Procedure and the potential that Bryce could receive a metal valve that would need to be replaced every three to five years, my friend began telling me about a child of a friend of his. The child also had a congenital heart condition and had multiple open heart surgeries. "Every time they have to go back in for another open heart surgery, everything is all gummed up in there and stuck together. It gets worse every time they have to re-open the chest cavity."

I wasn't really sure how to respond to this story. If it was supposed to make me feel better, it had the exact opposite effect. "Why would someone say that to a mother, fully knowing that I just finished explaining to him that my child may need multiple open heart surgeries?" I said, finishing my story to Doug.

"How did you handle your response?"

"The only thing I knew to do was make some excuse that I needed to get back to my office—he had stopped me in the hallway. I just wanted to end the conversation and get away from him."

"It is good that you removed yourself from the situation and didn't just stay and continue getting more upset," Doug responded. "I believe most people have good intentions, even if they may not know how to engage the filter on their mouth."

Next, we discussed things I could do to educate the people close to me about CHD so they can learn and better understand. I had never really posted on social media much before having Bryce, but that changed as I began sharing our story and information to create awareness around CHD. I found it was therapeutic for me and helped to lessen the number of times I had to explain that Bryce was not "cured" from this and "no, it is likely not his last surgery."

⬦⬦⬦

In November 2016, we were back at the cardiologist for another check-up. I asked my mother to come with me again because I had found myself forgetting some of the information the doctor would say. He liked to make sure I understood our next steps, so sometimes it was a lot of information to absorb. Even at forty-three years old, having my mother with me helped keep me calm. Bryce's echo in April showed his heart was slightly bigger, but it wasn't enough of a change to cause concern or do anything different at that time. The cardiologist said, "The leak has not changed, and the gradient is still at a level I am comfortable with. Taking all things into consideration, I am happy with Bryce's progress."

Fast forward to November; Bryce knew the routine, and he wasn't scared. He knew that there were no "ouchies" at the heart doctor. By now, he knew the drill almost better than the nurses. He hopped up on the table and laid down for her to place the EKG wires on his chest. When some fell off, he said, "I'll help you!" as he pressed the stickers back down. When the EKG was finished, he sat up and held out his arm for her to place the blood pressure cuff on. He said, "I know. It's going to give me a big hug."

The nurse laughed. "You've got this down pretty well, haven't you?"

Next, we moved to see the cardiologist for the physical exam, and Bryce asked, "Do I get to do the gel today?" He called the echocardiogram "the gel."

"Yes. Someone will be in to take you to the echo shortly." Then he turned to me and said, "We will talk after they are done."

The sonogram technician was so great with Bryce. "Bryce, what is your favorite movie?"

"Ronan."

She looked confused and said, "Hmm ... I haven't heard of that one."

I explained, "It is the movie, *Epic*.[2] Ronan is the character in the movie." She didn't know the movie but took the time to ask another tech if he had it, and what do you know ... he did!

*That was so kind of her to go out of her way like that. It makes the process so much easier if Bryce has something to distract him, especially now that he's getting older and does not want to stay still.*

Following the echo, the cardiologist came into the room to look at the pictures and talked to me and my mom. "Bryce's heart is dilated more than last time, but it is keeping up with his growth rate."

---

2   Chris Wedge, *Epic* (Blue Sky Studios, 20th Century Fox, Animation), 2013.

He showed me a chart of normal kids Bryce's age (without a heart issue) compared to Bryce. Bryce's heart was slightly above normal, but the change from April to November aligned with his growth. "We are watching to see if the change shows a huge spike, then we will want to do something. Bryce has more options available to him and is not strictly limited to the Ross Procedure."

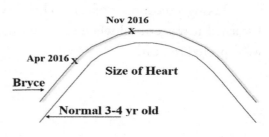

The Ross was the procedure Rob and I feared the most. This was the first time the cardiologist talked to me about a possible valve repair. When I had asked about a repair before, when Bryce was eight months old, he had told me, "It would be too risky." If the repair didn't work, then they would have to go to the Ross Procedure, which would have been two major surgeries that Bryce, as an infant, would have had to recover from.

"A repair would still be an open heart surgery; however, the recovery time would be faster and less harsh for Bryce," the doctor continued.

"What do they use for a repair?"

"They would use part of Bryce's own tissue to do the repair, so we don't have to worry about his heart rejecting it. Bryce's heart is growing and is closer to the size they have available if he should need a valve replacement."

"This is great news!" I said. "A repair sounds like a better option than having a metal valve that constantly needs to be replaced because it won't grow with him."

For the time being, the cardiologist was pleased with how energetic Bryce was, and his heart still looked stable, so things were status quo for now, and we would follow up again in six months. I was so grateful my mother went with me to this visit because I felt like the heart doctor gave me a lot of great information, but sometimes my mind was still processing one thing he said when he started telling me something else.

Taking a second set of ears to listen was a great idea. Soon after, I learned it was crucial when the news they delivered was not what we expected to hear.

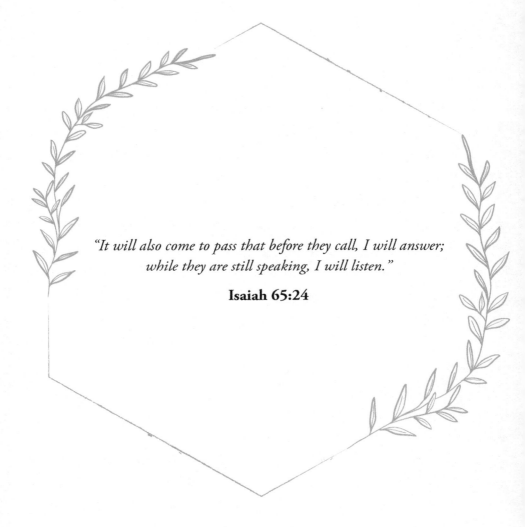

*"It will also come to pass that before they call, I will answer; while they are still speaking, I will listen."*

**Isaiah 65:24**

# 18

# Big Muscles Are Not Always Great

The nurse escorted us to the room where the echo technician was waiting. I had to catch my breath when we walked into the room. It was the same room we were in the day of Bryce's echo when he was in heart failure at five weeks old. I glanced at the corner of the room where I stood to call Rob to tell him the news when he was in the middle of planning his dad's funeral service. I'm not a superstitious person, but this room definitely did not bring back great memories for me.

It was Tuesday, April 11th, 2017. Bryce was now four years old. The echo was taking much longer than usual and was making me tense. I had brought my older sister, Tina, with me this time. I turned to ask her what time the echo had started. She confirmed that we started at 11:30 a.m. It was now 12:35 p.m. I tried asking the technician a question, and he was really intense. "I'm not going to talk if you don't mind, because I need to concentrate on him. Nothing personal. It's just hard trying to take pictures with him moving, so I need to concentrate."

I looked at my sister like, *What in the world?*

As he pressed the wand under Bryce's ribs, Bryce said, "You're pushing that really hard, you know!"

The tech replied, "I'm sorry, but you are a tough little kid. You're doing really great. I just have a little more to do; then I'll be done."

Finally, he finished, and the heart doctor came to look at the echo. "Bryce's left ventricle is enlarged again." He showed me the graph where Bryce's heart size was compared to other kids his size and age with normal hearts. I could see that this time Bryce's level on the chart was much higher than where it should be versus a normal level.

He explained, "The heart is a giant muscle; while it may be good to have large muscles in other places on your body, having large muscles in the heart is not a good thing. I want to present Bryce's case to my team of heart surgeons and specialists. I don't want to give my opinion until I talk to my team, which will be in two days. I will call you by the end of the week."

We had taken the kids camping that week, but that particular day was a dreary rainy day (kind of fitting for how I felt when I left the heart doctor's office), so we went to Tina's house to let Bryce and his cousin play.

Over the next several days, I prayed and prayed, *Dear God, please guide us and grant us Your grace through these unchartered waters. I pray You will guide the physicians and specialists to make the best decision for Bryce to give him the best chance at a long and healthy life.*

I found it difficult to keep my mind off the phone call I was waiting for and carried my phone everywhere with me. I was breaking my own rule about no electronics when we're camping. I had to explain to the kids that I was waiting for an important phone call from a doctor.

Rob and I waited until the kids fell asleep at night to talk about what the doctor might say. "I'm scared. I thought he wouldn't need another surgery until he was nine or ten," I confided to Rob.

"Try not to worry about it until we know for sure if they want to do surgery. Worrying isn't going to change anything."

I tried to look up as much information as possible about valve repair in children and the Ross Procedure so I could prepare a list of questions for the surgeons. I searched the social media groups for ideas on explaining surgery to a child, if that was the route we had to take. I worried he would be scared when he woke from surgery to find a scar on his chest. I fell asleep every night praying, *God, be with us; watch over our son; strengthen my faith; give me hope that everything will turn out the way You intend; and help guide us to trustworthy surgeons who will help our little boy.*

I found peace in reading Isaiah 41:10:

> "Do not fear, for I am with you; Do not be afraid, for I am your God. I will strengthen you, I will also help you, I will also uphold you with My righteous right hand."

◇◇◇◇◇

**O**n Thursday evening, as promised, I received the call I had been awaiting. The kids were on the playground at the campgrounds when my phone rang. The cardiologist said, "I presented Bryce's case to my team earlier today. They all agreed it's time to do something. The benefits of waiting no longer outweigh the risks of the harm that would come to Bryce if his left ventricle continued to enlarge. It isn't an urgent need, but we can't wait another year. You'll need to call the office in the morning to ask for an appointment with the heart surgeons."

A week after I got the call telling me Bryce had been referred to the heart surgeons, Rob and I were in the waiting room with Bryce and my mother. The cardiologist told us to bring Bryce with us in case the surgeons wanted to evaluate him, so we brought Grandma with us to help with Bryce while we were trying to talk with the surgeons. We were escorted to a large conference room, where we met two heart surgeons. One is a complex neonatal congenital heart specialist from the Cleveland Clinic, and one is a cardiac surgery doctor affiliated with the children's hospital where we take Bryce. The surgeons began our meeting by explaining that Bryce's left ventricle had gradually been getting bigger. "His Z-score is now at 4.7, which is putting such a strain on his heart that we can no longer continue waiting."

The whole time I was sitting there, I was thinking, *Please don't say you want to do the Ross Procedure. Please, not the Ross!*

They drew pictures on a board to help explain and were extremely patient with our questions. The cardiologist from the Cleveland Clinic, Dr. Stewart, told us, "The leak in the valve is the main concern right now. It is possible we could go in and see that the leak is being caused by a hole that could be mended using Bryce's own tissue or a small patch. This would be the repair option, but it would only be done if we are more than 90 percent confident that the repair will be successful and allow his heart to have a good, sustainable function."

Next, he went on to explain the Ross Procedure. My shoulders dropped, and I immediately felt myself tense up. He said, "We would resort to the Ross Procedure if we decide a repair is not feasible. That decision would be made on the operating table."

At that point in the conversation, I was trying to remind myself to breathe. *I know all about the Ross Procedure and how it has been successful with moving the pulmonary valve to the aortic valve,* I thought. *I want to know what their plans are for the pulmonary replacement!*

Everything I could find on children was that it would be replaced with a metal valve. Metal valves mean blood thinners. It means open heart surgeries every three years. Rob asked the question he knew I was burning to ask. "Will it be replaced with a metal valve?"

We were speechless when the response came back, "No, we do not use metal valves in little kids; one, because of the need for anticoagulants and two, the difficulty in regulating the dosage of blood thinners in such little kids due to their rapid growth. We will be using a donor valve for the homograph, or pulmonary replacement. We will use a slightly bigger valve so that as Bryce grows, the valve will stretch and give him more time before a follow-up surgery would be necessary."

*This is such great news! No metal valve! No blood thinners and possibly a longer time between replacement surgery!* Rob and I asked about the replacement surgery.

Dr. Stewart told us, "If the homograph needs replaced, we can do that through a catheter. We go in through an artery in the leg and swap out the valves. There are medical engineers working every day to collapse the homograph to a smaller size so they can fit it through a cath in infants."

*This is even better news!! This could mean that the follow-up surgery would not need to be open heart surgery! No going through scar tissue where it's all gummed up, and no messing with trying to re-open his chest cavity!*

Rob asked, "Do we have to wait for a donor valve, and if so, how long?"

To our surprise, they said, "No, we have valves in a tank, a freezer, right now. Since our hospitals work together, we have access to both tanks, which means there is no need to wait."

Dr. Stewart explained, "When people donate their organs, if their entire heart isn't a match or can't be used, then they use the valves. The valves can be kept in the freezer for five years, so it's really up to you when you want to schedule the surgery. It can't wait too long, but you have time to schedule it around when your family can take a week to dedicate to living at the hospital and six weeks to care for Bryce as he heals."

"How long until Bryce can return to normal activity?" I asked.

"At a minimum, he will need to stay out of preschool for six weeks. No roughhousing and risk re-opening his chest." Then Dr.

Stewart further explained, "It takes six weeks for the chest to close back up and three months to fully heal. The Ross Procedure has had a higher success rate in kids where their biological heart disease is stenosis. Although the leak is Bryce's main problem right now, it was a manmade defect caused by the balloon cath he had as an infant. Bryce was born with aortic stenosis, so if he has the Ross Procedure, his success rate is pretty positive. Bryce will stay in the hospital for a week and come out of surgery on a ventilator similar to his balloon cath; however, he may come off the ventilator on the day of surgery, or it could be the next day. It really depends on the kid, and each case is different. It will depend on how Bryce is doing and how the surgery goes."

When Rob and I walked out of the surgeon's office, I felt like a huge weight had been lifted from my shoulders. *Bryce will actually have a shot at a long, healthy, and normal childhood if they do this surgery, and all the things I agonized over did not come to fruition.*

On the drive home, I said a silent prayer. *Thank you, Father, for sending Bryce to these surgeons, who are going to give him a chance at a normal childhood. I am so grateful that I will not have to watch my son endure surgery after multiple open heart surgery. I ask that You watch over Bryce. Cover him with the protection of Your blood. Help us keep him healthy for his upcoming surgery. Please give Rob and me the strength we need to help him through this. In Jesus' name. Amen.*

*"Cast all your anxiety on Him, because He cares about you."*

**1 Peter 5:7**

# Lay Your Burdens at the Cross

Six weeks. Bryce's surgery had been scheduled six weeks after the meeting with the heart surgeons—six weeks for me to prepare. Six weeks to keep Bryce healthy, so surgery won't be rescheduled. Six weeks to allow Bryce to do the things he will not be able to do for most of his summer. You might ask why we chose to have the surgery at the peak of summer when they told us it was not urgent. Deciding on the date actually took quite a bit of thought, and many factors had to be considered. The most important was the availability of Dr. Stewart to come to our local hospital. He and the surgeon from the local children's hospital would both perform the surgery (one on each side of the heart), so we needed to choose a date when both of their schedules were free.

Having the surgery at the local hospital also meant less travel for family members who would want to come and visit Bryce while in the hospital. It meant less travel for the follow-up visits as well. The second largest factor was my availability to take time off work. I did not have six weeks of vacation, but I had a flexible and very understanding boss. Taking several weeks off all at once would pose a challenge to our department, so it was mutually beneficial for me to take a full week of vacation the week Bryce would be in the hospital, and then I would take a combination of vacation days and work from home throughout the next three weeks.

For the last two weeks of Bryce's restrictions, I would lean on family members to watch Bryce while I had to go into the office. This hybrid working scenario was considered trail-blazing in 2017, and I knew I was fortunate to have a boss who had confidence that I would do the work and not take advantage of his trust. I was also willing to be flexible in choosing a time of the year that was not extremely busy with operations finance since we were not as heavily involved in strategic planning as I had been when I was supporting the business team. The final deciding point to have the surgery in the summer was due to the lower chances of Bryce getting sick. Four-year-olds (at least our four-year-old) still need to be reminded not to put their hands in their mouth after touching a doorknob, a restaurant counter, or after playing with toys that other children have touched. Rob and I knew our best chance of getting Bryce to his surgery date healthy was to schedule it in June.

Now that we had a date on the calendar, I was tested again in my ability to focus on the things within my control. I will not lie; I failed more often than I succeeded. I was filled with worry. I did a lot of crying in the shower to hide my fear from the kids. If ever there was a time I wished I could trade places with one of my kids, this was it. If I could take this for him, to shield him from any of the pain, I would lay down and bear every bit of it … if I could.

I plunged myself into researching, reading, and finding everything I could to help us prepare. I found solace in reading stories from Heart Moms about their kids who had the Ross Procedure to fix their valve.

"Heart Mom." I've accepted this title. I proudly wear that badge for my little heart warrior.

One Heart Mom shared that her son had the Ross when he was five, and her child was able to play soccer and had played ice hockey for eight years. He is now twenty-eight! Another child had the Ross at four months old, the pulmonary valve replaced at eight years old, and is now seventeen and doing well. I asked questions in the social media groups for guidance on how to prepare for surgery and what to take with us to the hospital. Some parents recommended buying button-up shirts and pajamas because, they explained, "Bryce will have sternal restrictions after surgery."

I didn't even know what sternal restrictions were until a mom shared with me, "My child was extremely sore after his surgery. Raising his arms will be painful, so t-shirts are not a good idea."

I sent a question to Bryce's cardiology team to ask about sternal restrictions and found out that Bryce will not be permitted to push, pull, swing a bat, climb, or even push himself off the floor or couch using his arms for a minimum of six weeks. "No pushing, pulling, or swinging?" I read out loud. "That means no Nerf guns; no play swords; no baseball; and no swing set. We're going to have to rope off the play fort," I told Rob.

"I'm worried about keeping him from jumping off the couch, let alone the playset."

"I think we have an extremely long six weeks ahead of us," I said.

The response from the cardiologist's office also explained, "You will not be able to pick your child up from under his arms." *I had not even thought about that.*

"How are we going to pick him up?" I asked.

They responded, "You can lift him from under his butt. His ribs will be healing, so picking him up by his arms is absolutely out of the question."

We were now a month from Bryce's surgery. I found myself looking at Bryce and thinking that soon, I would not remember what he looked like without a scar on his chest. It broke my heart. I would wake up with my mind racing. I couldn't shut it off. If I wasn't worrying about the actual surgery and what Bryce had to go through, then I was worrying about how I would keep him from overexerting himself after the surgery. I would wake at three in the morning and end up picking up my phone to research. I got lost in reading about what they have to do during the Ross Procedure: "The child would be hooked up to something called a bypass machine during the surgery. The machine would act as your child's heart and lungs during the procedure, which could last five to six hours. Once they have removed the aortic valve, replaced it with the pulmonary valve, and placed a donor valve in the pulmonary position, they will begin removing the child from the heart-lung machine, and their heart will begin beating on its own. The breastbone will be put back together with wires, and then the breast muscle will be sutured."

These are the things that kept me up at night. *Oh, my poor Bryce,* I thought.

After church services one day, I was talking to my pastor about my struggle to keep the worry at bay. She suggested that I write a letter to God to get all my worries on paper. What I share with you now is my letter to God, as is, with every raw emotion poured out at His feet.

*Dear Father in Heaven,*

*My thoughts lately have become so overclouded with worry, fear, and nervousness about my son's upcoming heart surgery. I have researched and educated myself about the procedure, as well as the surgeons, so I am fully aware of what to expect. Both surgeons have excellent credentials and years of experience, but I can't stop the fear of the "what-ifs." This is where I know I have to turn to my faith in You and my trust in Your Son, Jesus Christ, to carry my son through this.*

*I know You were with us when Bryce's heart started to fail four years ago, and You have never left his side during this journey.*

*I ask for Your help, dear God, to help me lay my worries and fears at the foot of the cross. Please help me put all my effort into loving my son and giving him the care, love, and support he will need to heal and recover. When You see me start to falter or my mind begins to turn back to fear, please help me feel Your presence and know that You have not left our side.*

*I pray that You will guide the surgeons' hands during the surgery and help keep their minds focused and their hands steady. I pray that the surgery nurses, anesthesiologists, and support staff will all care for Bryce in the best possible way to give him the top-notched quality care he will need through surgery and recovery. Dear God, please bless my son with the blood of Jesus Christ. Help him to be strong so he can pull through the surgery without any complications. I pray that his little heart will continue to be strong and his left ventricle will continue keeping up with the extra work needed to sustain the leak in his valve as we await the surgery he needs to maintain his energetic and spirited personality.*

*God, I ask You to give me the strength, patience, and knowledge I will need to take care of and support my son through this. Help me pay attention to the instructions we are given by his doctors and nurses, so I can properly care for Bryce. Let me be attentive to Bryce's needs and be perceptive to his pain, so I will know when he's not feeling well and in need of comfort or relief. I pray that as we are all focused on Bryce's pain and recovery that we continue to care for and love our daughter, Reyna. I pray I will be patient with her through all that she is having to watch her brother go through. I need to remember that she is only eight years old and will probably be worried or scared for her brother. As her mother, I pray You will help me remember that and pay attention if she needs someone to talk to or a shoulder to cry on.*

*Lord, please bless our family. Help us to pull together to be there for each other and for Bryce. Help us to show love, kindness, and understanding over anger, doubt, or fear. I ask this in the name of the Father, the Son, and the Holy Ghost. In Jesus' name. Amen.*

This letter to God helped me set my fears down so I could move forward. Over the next three weeks, I kept my focus on the things that I could gather in advance of surgery to help make Bryce's recovery time more comfortable. These are the things I had control over, the things I needed to spend my time and energy on and stop dwelling on things beyond my control.

- I bought some button-up shirts, travel games, and coloring books to take with us to the hospital.
- I also found a lap desk with a cushion under it. It's made to hold on your lap and has a cup holder. I hoped Bryce could use it to avoid lifting his arms to color at the coffee table.
- Again, I turned to friends and family on social media for support. I was working on a song playlist to use while at the hospital, and I asked for suggestions. I was looking for uplifting music. Nothing that was going to instill fear or shake my faith.

A friend of mine suggested the song "Even If" by MercyMe. I found the video with the "Song & Testimony by Bart Millard."[3] It was perfect and became number one on my recently played playlist leading up to and after the surgery. If you have never listened to this song, I urge you to go find it. Bart Millard's testimony and faith are beautiful and exemplify everything I felt during that time. He talked about a friend who asked how his son (a diabetic) was doing, and the friend stopped him and said, "Let me pray for you." The notion that Bart had not thought of praying for his son hit him wrong that particular day. He knew that was not what his friend meant; she simply wanted to express love for him and his son by appealing to

---

[3] "MercyMe - Even If 'Song & Testimony' Live!," YouTube (YouTube, April 11, 2017), https://www.youtube.com/watch?v=WHosmHnOrb8.

God to help them. This is sometimes what I catch myself feeling when someone tells me they will pray for Bryce.

I get what Bart was saying. I had been praying every night since my son was diagnosed with this disease. *Why would God answer someone else's prayer and not mine?*

Then I was reading my Bible and came to Matthew 18:20:

> "For where two or three have gathered together in My name, I am there in their midst."

That was when it hit me. *One of the best things I can do for Bryce is ask people to pray. Between our family, church family, friends, and my extended family's church family, we could have hundreds of voices lifting Bryce to God in prayer.*

*"Do not be anxious about anything, but in everything by prayer and pleading with thanksgiving let your requests be made known to God. And the peace of God, which surpasses all comprehension, will guard your hearts and minds in Christ Jesus."*

**Philippians 4:6–7**

# 20

# Siblings Suffer Too

The Asian Sun Intra-School Tournament for Taekwondo was scheduled for May 13th, 2017. Bryce wanted to participate in the Tiger Tot Olympics because his sister, Reyna, was competing in the tournament for older kids. Rob and I decided we would let him participate. His cardiologist had given Bryce the green light to take Taekwondo last year as long as we listened when Bryce told us he needed a break. We were not to push him and needed to let him rest when he needed it. Bryce had taken part in the tournament last year, so we knew the instructors let the Tiger Tots go at their own pace. Bryce was super excited that he got a trophy and a medal at the tournament. Reyna did very well at the tournament, too, and earned gold medals for forms and board breaking.

The following weekend, Bryce had received an invitation to two different birthday parties for kids in his preschool. Normally, I would not allow the kids to go to parties on both Saturday and Sunday, but with Bryce's upcoming surgery, I wanted to let him live life and do the things he would not be able to do while he was recovering. I wanted to see him laughing and playing with his friends, and, for a weekend, I wanted to forget about surgeries and CHD. I just wanted Bryce to be a kid.

While I was sitting at the bowling alley watching one of the birthday parties, the mother of one of Reyna's friends was there, and she stopped to ask me how we were all holding up.

"We're doing as best as can be expected."

"How is Reyna handling everything?" she asked.

"She has been so good with Bryce lately. They've been playing and getting along better than ever."

As we talked, something occurred to me: I had not yet told Reyna's teacher about Bryce's upcoming surgery. That evening, I drafted an email to Reyna's teacher to let her know what was going on with Bryce. I told her about Bryce's surgery, which was now a week and a half away. I wanted her to be aware in case she noticed any changes in Reyna on the day of the surgery or the days leading up to it. I wrote:

> *Please reach out to me if you notice a change in Reyna's work, participation in class, or demeanor. We went through something similar when Reyna was in preschool; while we have a better idea of what to expect this time around, I also remember that those weeks were very hard on Reyna. It was hard with our family being separated, with Bryce and me at the hospital and Reyna and her dad at home. Rob will bring Reyna up to the hospital to see us after he gets off work, but then she may get home late and be tired the next day for school. We are doing our best at home to keep things as normal as possible, but I also know that kids have a way of sensing when something is worrying parents, despite our best efforts.*

I was caught off guard when I read the response from the teacher the next day:

> *I am so sorry for what all of you are going through. I have already noticed a slight difference with Reyna, but nothing*

*to be alarmed about. She's been a little distracted and more talkative to friends, and I've had to talk to her a few times over the past two weeks. This explains a lot. It also explains why she is wanting to write about Bryce for every personal narrative. I feel bad because I told her she needed to switch up her topics. Thank you for sharing what's going on at home. I will keep an eye on her for you. If you'd like, I can see if the school counselor is available to talk to her. If there is anything I can do to help, please let me know. Best wishes for you and your family.*

I wanted to kick myself for being so blind and not reaching out to the teacher earlier! *How could I not have noticed that all of Reyna's narratives coming home from school were about Bryce? I should have learned from Bryce's first heart surgery when Reyna blamed herself and thought she had made Bryce sick! At least I know now, and I can talk with Reyna about any concerns or questions she has.*

That night, I sat by Reyna's bedside and asked, "Do you have questions about Bryce's surgery?"

"How long will you be at the hospital? Will it be as long as last time?"

"The doctors said it would probably be a week. As long as Bryce is doing well after surgery, he will be able to come home. Bryce is not going to be allowed to do certain things when he comes home, and we will have to keep an eye out that he doesn't try to play with his Nerf guns or climb the playset."

Reyna asked, "Will Bryce be allowed to swim in the pool?"

"No, at least not until he's released."

"I won't swim in the pool either because I don't want to make Bryce feel bad that he can't swim too."

I told her, "That is very kind of you. Maybe you can swim when Bryce takes his two-hour naps."

"I wish Bryce didn't have to have so many surgeries. I think I would be scared if I had to have heart surgery."

I reassured her, "The heart surgeons that will be doing Bryce's surgery are very good at what they do. They do these types of surgeries at least a hundred times a year for little kids, so Bryce will be in very good hands. Bryce has God watching over him, too."

That night we prayed together, and Reyna asked God to "take care of my brother and let his surgery go good so Mommy and Bryce can come home."

One of the most significant lessons I've learned throughout our CHD journey as a family is that it is also important to keep in mind the effects it has on siblings. As in any family expecting a new baby, we knew we would have the transition period as Reyna learned to deal with no longer being the baby of the family. Reyna's older siblings were eleven and sixteen years older than her, so she was used to having the full attention of her parents and siblings. What we didn't prepare for was how to manage the transition in conjunction with a child having a congenital heart condition.

We didn't prepare for Reyna's mother being away from her for an entire week, caring for a brother she had barely met. Then, when the family was finally home and together, we had to keep Bryce from crying and overworking his heart. This meant more attention being pulled away from Reyna. Trying to keep a hungry baby from crying while you wait for the bottle to warm is a challenge, to say the least. Or managing to give a baby a bath without allowing them to cry when you take them out of the warm bath is no small feat. Bath time became a whole new learning curve since we were not allowed to let Bryce cry. He loved being in the warm water and would splash and play. The moment we took him out of the bathwater, he would wail and scream. My heart would race, and my hands would shake as I frantically worked to get him wrapped in a towel, into his pajamas, and then quickly settled in to feed him so he would calm down. I learned it helped to put his towel and pajamas in the dryer on low for a little while to warm them up slightly. Rob would trade places with me and stay with Bryce in the bath while I ran to grab his nice warm clothes to have ready for him as soon as we took him out of the bath.

It was difficult to explain to a four-year-old child that you have to stop reading the bedtime story in the middle of the book because the baby needs his diaper changed, and "I can't make him wait." When Reyna was in kindergarten, her school participated in the Kids Heart Challenge with the American Heart Association. We found this function provided Reyna an opportunity to feel like she could help her brother. When Reyna ended up the top fundraiser in the entire school that year, she came home and said, "Now we can get Bryce a new heart, Mom!"

Of course, I explained to her that the fundraiser didn't work that way, but it helped raise money for medical research to help kids like Bryce. These were lessons we had to learn along the way. I praised God for letting my daughter speak up when she was carrying the burden of guilt that was not hers to carry. I thanked the Lord for putting me in the path of the mother of Reyna's friend, who prompted me to reach out to Reyna's teacher. While I'd like to say I've become a professional at paying attention to my children's feelings, I know that I still miss a lot, but the key is to keep talking to them. Keep listening and, most importantly, keep telling them they are loved.

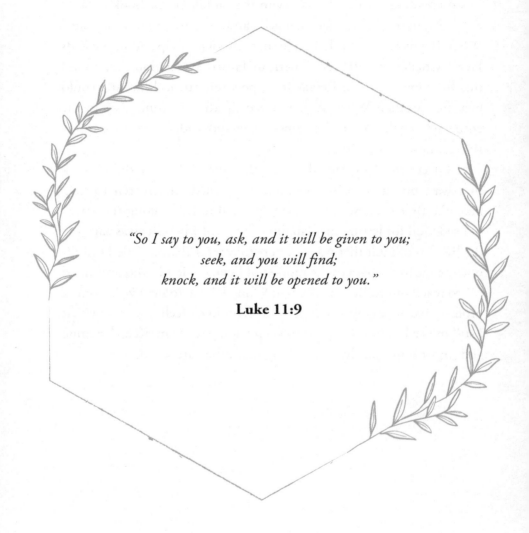

*"So I say to you, ask, and it will be given to you;*
*seek, and you will find;*
*knock, and it will be opened to you."*

**Luke 11:9**

# Badge of Courage

A full week of thunderstorms and heavy rain foiled our plans for Memorial Day weekend. We were supposed to take a camping trip as a last mini-vacation before Bryce's big surgery on June 1st, but unpredictable Ohio weather caused us to cancel. The campgrounds were a sopping muddy mess, so we took the kids to a family picnic on Sunday and let them visit with their cousins.

I had Memorial Day off and was using the quiet day to pack and get laundry caught up, since I would be at the hospital with Bryce for a week. I heard a noise coming from the bathroom and it sounded like someone calling for me. I knocked on the door to see which one of the kids it was and if they were okay. Bryce answered back, "Could you get me new shorts?"

"Did you wait too long to go to the bathroom and have an accident?" I asked.

"No ... I didn't pee."

I ran to grab new shorts and underwear and handed them through the door. Bryce slid his soiled clothes to me, and I could see what was wrong. When he came out, I asked him if his stomach hurt, and Bryce said, "No."

*Don't panic,* I told myself. *This could just be a fluke.*

Bryce went back to playing and then proceeded to go through three pairs of underwear in two hours. "What's wrong, Bryce? Do you feel okay?" I asked nervously.

"I feel okay, but every time I think I need to fart, then I have to run to the restroom to check."

"Are you having watery stools when you go to the bathroom?"

"Yes."

My head started going into panic mode. *Oh, my goodness! Not now! His surgery is in three days! They will make us reschedule!* The thought of another six weeks of waiting and all the anxiety of worrying was too much for me to wrap my head around. I was supposed to go to work on Tuesday, but ended up calling my boss to let him know what was going on with Bryce.

He said it was okay for me to work from home. I called Bryce's heart doctor's office to update them. The nurse called me back that afternoon and asked, "How is Bryce doing? Has he had a fever?"

"He hasn't had a fever. Today when he went to the restroom, everything was normal," I answered.

"It was probably just something he ate. Keep an eye on him to watch for any fever, and call us back if anything changes."

I was supposed to work a half-day on Wednesday and take vacation the other half. My mom agreed to watch Bryce instead of sending him to preschool that day. We didn't want to chance sending him to school and exposing him to anything else, since whatever was going on Monday had finally cleared up. We figured it was probably from all the watermelon Bryce had eaten at the picnic on Sunday afternoon. Bryce was excited to stay at Grandma's house for the day because he loved to ride around and help Papa do chores in his utility vehicle, and it also meant he could see his sissy get on and off the bus (something he always loved to do).

When Reyna returned from school, we went home to have dinner and let the kids play. We ate a little later that evening, since Bryce wasn't allowed any solid food after midnight. When it was getting closer to bedtime, Reyna told Bryce goodnight, and then I took her back to my mom's. She was going to spend the night at Grandma's house because we had to be at the hospital by seven-thirty in the morning, and Reyna still had a week left of the school year.

I had been trying all week to finish packing our bags for the hospital, but on the night before surgery, I was still gathering things I had forgotten to pack. The hospital had told us, "Bryce can bring his favorite blanket and toy with him, but anything going into the operating room would need washed."

I waited until Bryce was asleep and then slipped his Simba blanket from his arms so I could wash it. Bryce's Grandma Ripley had made him a Star Wars blanket and brought it over the day before his surgery. His grandmother is to sewing machines as Julia Child was to cooking. She made a beautiful blanket with velvet royal blue material on one side, and a soft cotton Star Wars material on the other. Bryce wanted to take the Star Wars blanket with him to surgery, so I was washing that too. They had told us he could only take one, but I washed them both in case he changed his mind about the blanket he had settled on.

Bryce also wanted to take his favorite stuffed animals, "Jack" the turtle and "Sven" the reindeer. As I washed the stuffed animals and blankets, I unpacked his bag and went through the checklist again to ensure I had everything. This was probably the fifth time I had rechecked the list. I was nervous, so I knew I would forget something. I remembered to pack his button-up pajamas, Lightning McQueen slippers, ChapStick, and tablet. By the time I got the blankets and toys out of the dryer and packed up, it was one-thirty in the morning when I finally laid my head on the pillow to pray.

*Father in Heaven, please help the doctors and nurses have clarity of mind to focus on my son's surgery in the morning. Let their hands be steady and move with skill and precision to allow the surgery to be a great success that will sustain my son for a long and healthy life. Please help guide Rob and me so that our faces do not show fear. Grant us the courage to be strong for our son. I ask this in Jesus' name. Amen.*

I felt like I had just closed my eyes when my alarm startled me awake at 5 o'clock on the morning of Bryce's surgery. I showered and packed the remainder of toiletries I was taking and then made coffee. I had decided I wasn't going to eat breakfast since Bryce couldn't eat anything, but with only having four hours of sleep, I allowed myself the coffee. Bryce woke up at 6:30. He was looking for Reyna and started crying when I reminded him she had spent the night at Grandma's. He said, "I miss her. Can we go see her?"

I knew Reyna had taken the iPad with her, so I tried to FaceTime her to see if they were awake. She answered, and Bryce was happy he got to say good morning to Reyna, Grandma, Papa, and Aunt Cindy (my mom's sister). I told Reyna I would FaceTime with her later that night when she was home from school, and we said our goodbyes because it was time to go.

Bryce was quiet on the car ride to the hospital. He watched the iPad on the way and didn't ask a lot of questions about where we were going. We had already explained to him he was going to have surgery so they could help his heart and that I was planning to stay at the hospital with him. Every once in a while, Bryce looked up from the iPad and asked, "You won't leave the hospital until I leave, right, Mom?"

I would answer, "That's right. I'm not leaving without you."

We arrived at the hospital and checked in at the outpatient surgery waiting room. We didn't have to wait. They called someone, and she came straight out to get us. She led us to a room and handed us some hospital pajamas to put on Bryce. Rob was helping Bryce get his pants off when I heard Bryce say, "Why do I have to take off my underwear?"

I explained, "They don't want anything tight on you, so they'd like you to put on the nice comfy loose pajamas."

As Rob helped Bryce switch his pants, I could hear quiet sniffles coming from Rob. As much as I wanted to cry myself, I knew if one of us started, we both would, and Bryce needed us to be strong right now. We could not let him see fear or worry in his parents' eyes. I whispered to Rob, "Please don't do that right now."

Rob wiped his face, took a breath, and continued helping Bryce change. I honestly was not being heartless. My heart was breaking too. The nice thing about having each other was being able to help hold the other up when one of us started to stumble. It was the only way we both could help each other and help Bryce through this whole ordeal. Once Bryce was in the hospital pajamas, we waited for them to prep him for surgery.

The anesthesiologist, two heart surgeons, a nurse practitioner, and the child life specialist all came to see us and check on Bryce. Pastor Susan was allowed to come back to see Bryce, and we all prayed together for a successful surgery and for God never to leave Bryce's side. A nurse came in to ask which blanket and toy Bryce was taking with him to surgery. He chose the Star Wars blanket and his little turtle. As more people came into the room to ask for insurance information, explain risks, and what to expect during surgery, Bryce kept asking us to turn up the television because he couldn't hear over our talking. It was comforting to me that he was so relaxed and calm, and at the same time, a little strange because we were supposed to be comforting him.

The child life specialist asked Bryce, "Want to take a walk with me, buddy?" This was the test to see how well he would do with separation from us. He did great.

In fact, when they walked down to get his height and weight, he turned to wave at me and said, "Bye, Mom!"

Shocked, I said, "What? I'm not leaving yet! I better get hugs before you go!" Then we walked back to the room so Bryce could pick which flavor he wanted in his mask. They put flavored ChapStick in the mask so the kids smell it instead of the anesthetic.

The child life specialist asked Rob and me, "Have you explained the surgery and the scar to Bryce?"

I answered, "We've told him that the doctors are going to fix his heart, but we haven't really explained the scar. I didn't think that was necessary."

"One of you needs to explain it to him before he goes into surgery. We prefer it comes from a parent, but if you don't explain it to him, I will."

I took a deep breath and turned to Bryce. "Do you remember why you are here?" I asked him.

"For surgery."

"Yes. Those two doctors that were just in here are going to help your heart feel better. When you come out of surgery, you are going to have your very own superhero badge right on your chest. It's going to show everybody how brave you are."

Bryce thought for a minute, looked directly at me, and said, "Are you just kidding?"

I answered, "No. You will have a little line right here," as I motioned to the middle of his chest. "That is going to be your very own badge of courage."

Bryce was happy with that response and went on watching cartoons.

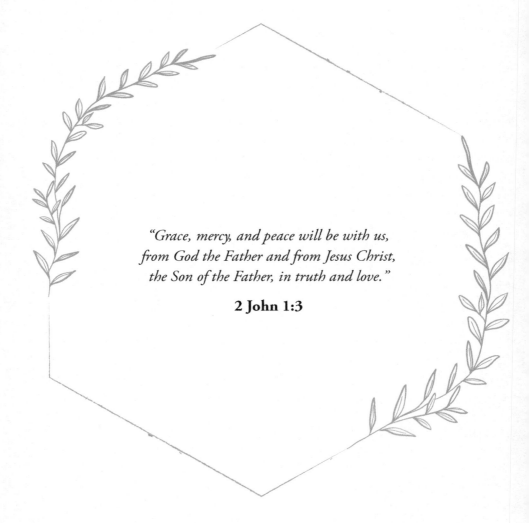

*"Grace, mercy, and peace will be with us,
from God the Father and from Jesus Christ,
the Son of the Father, in truth and love."*

**2 John 1:3**

# 22

# Leaving It to God

Soon, the time came when the nurse said they were ready for Bryce. This was a different nurse, and she told Bryce, "You can take both blankets and both stuffed animals back with you." Bryce picked up Jack, Sven, his Simba blanket, and the Star Wars blanket from Grandma Ripley, gave Rob and me one last hug and kiss, and we watched our four-year-old walk down the hallway toward the operating room. He looked so tiny, so innocent, as he walked away from us. I took comfort in knowing he did not seem afraid, and the nurse was letting him walk at his pace, so he didn't feel rushed.

As they walked out of sight, Pastor Susan, Rob, and I turned to find our way to the surgery waiting room. They had provided a patient number that we were supposed to be able to use to follow the status on the waiting room board, but the only ones provided were "surgery, recovery, or pre-surgery." Thankfully, the physician's assistant, Fran, who was assisting in the surgery, would come to the waiting room to provide updates throughout the surgery.

Surgery started at 8:40 a.m., and our first update came at 10:15. Fran told us, "They have him on the bypass machine, and they are looking at the valve to see what they are deciding to do."

While we were waiting, I was providing updates to extended family through group chats. I updated my group chat to tell them they were deciding which way to go: repair or replacement. My sister Rachel asked, "Which one are we praying for?"

I responded, "We are leaving it up to God."

I had just memorized Psalm 23; someone at church recently taught the kids to say it using a rosary. I was trying to remember it as we waited for the answer on how we were moving forward.

> *The LORD is my shepherd, I will not be in need. He lets me lie down in green pastures; He leads me beside quiet waters. He restores my soul; He guides me in the paths of righteousness for the sake of His name. Even though I walk through the valley of the shadow of death, I fear no evil, for You are with me; Your rod and Your staff, they comfort me. You prepare a table before me in the presence of my enemies; You have anointed my head with oil; My cup overflows. Certainly goodness and faithfulness will follow me all the days of my life, And my dwelling will be in the house of the LORD forever.*

Meanwhile, my mom had texted to tell me she and Reyna had said a prayer for Bryce and the doctors this morning. She said, "After I added the doctors to the prayer, Reyna told me, 'Don't worry, Grandma. They do hundreds of these surgeries every year, so they know what to do.'" Mom thought that it was so sweet of Reyna to comfort her.

"I'm glad to hear this," I said, "because I had told Reyna that about the surgeons one day when she was worrying about Bryce. I'm glad to know that she was listening."

At 10:35 a.m., Fran came back with another update: "Valve replacement." They decided to move forward with the Ross Procedure.

The next update came at 11:20 a.m. "Bryce's new homograft [donor valve] and his autograft [his pulmonary valve transplanted to his aortic valve] are in place. The two surgeons are monitoring the two valves and doing a diligent overview to ensure they don't see any leaks or issues before they take Bryce off the bypass."

Two hours later, Fran came to tell us, "Bryce is off the bypass machine, and his heart is beating on its own. They are in the process of closing him up, and you should get to talk with the surgeons soon."

*Thank you, Father, for watching over Bryce and the surgeons,* I silently prayed.

**H**alf an hour later, we were in a tiny conference room waiting for the surgeons to come and talk to Rob and me. The surgeons arrived and told us the surgery went very well. Dr. Stewart said, "We took a look at his aortic valve and immediately knew a repair would not make sense. There were barely two flaps as we had previously thought, and, by our definition, it would be considered a unicuspid valve. The replacement was the best possible outcome. His pulmonary valve was as beautiful as his aortic valve was ugly, so we made the switch."

Rob asked the surgeons, "Will this surgery mean Bryce will have more energy than before?"

The surgeon smiled and said, "Sorry. I did my job."

Rob smiled, thanked the surgeons, and then asked, "What size valve were you able to use for Bryce's pulmonary valve?"

I was thankful Rob thought to ask this. My mind was just so relieved to hear everything was a success, I wasn't thinking about what questions to ask.

"Bryce's valve measured 15mm, and we were able to use an 18mm valve."

"What size does an adult valve measure?" asked Rob.

"About 24mm. It's possible that Bryce's new aortic valve could very well carry him through his entire life. Since it is his valve and his cells, it will grow with him. The homograft will stretch some, but it won't grow with him. Since we were able to use a bigger size, this will allow him more time to grow, and he likely will not need a replacement until he's much older. By that time, he probably would be a good candidate for the melody valve."

I made a mental note to research the melody valve. They told us Bryce was being moved to recovery, and we could see him in about an hour and a half. So we thanked the surgeons for answering our questions and returned to our family in the waiting room.

By now, Bryce's grandparents, Aunt Liza, and Pastor Susan were still waiting to hear that Bryce was in recovery and doing well. We updated them on the news from the surgeons as we waited for Bryce to be moved to his room. I kept watching the clock. "They said an hour and a half," I told Rob. "What could be taking them so long?"

Time seemed to stand still. Finally, I couldn't take waiting anymore. "I'm going to go see how things are going and ask when we can see him." I stood to leave the waiting room.

I pushed the button to the ICU area and asked the lady at the desk for a status on Bryce Ripley. "Are you Mom?" she asked.

"Yes, I am."

She pointed to a room behind me and said, "Around the corner." I turned to walk toward the room she had directed me to and noticed there were a lot of people in that room. I couldn't see the bed because they were all standing around it. One of the nurses moved, and I could see Bryce lying there. I stopped in the hallway and stared without making a sound.

Someone touched my arm and said, "Can we see him?"

I pointed in the room's direction. I couldn't talk. I was trying to swallow that lump in my throat again. Tears softly filled the corners of my eyes as I followed Rob into the room. I was trying to process all the wires going into my little boy. I couldn't tell where one started, and the other ended. There were so many!

Dr. Stewart was stooped over on the other side of the bed, looking at some type of box that had a tube attached to Bryce just below his rib cage. The box was nearly full of a bronze-colored substance (I learned later this was the wound drain tube). As he stood up, I could clearly see the concern on his face. He explained, "Bryce's blood pressure is higher than we want."

I asked, "What caused that?"

"They were trying to take a chest x-ray before they brought him to recovery; Bryce sat straight up and tried to crawl off the table!"

"Oh, my goodness!" I exclaimed. "He tried to crawl off the table while he was attached to all of these tubes and the ventilator? Wasn't he still sedated?"

"Yes, his back must have hit that cold metal plate they laid him on, and it brought him right out of anesthesia. I wanted Bryce's systolic blood pressure kept under 110 for two hours after surgery to give the valve time to adjust. The drainage from his surgery is also draining faster than we would like. Bryce trying to crawl off the table likely caused the drainage flow to spike. We are trying to get him calmed down and hopefully get him to sleep. You can visit him, but we'd like you to keep it to two at a time. We really need him to rest, so don't try to wake him up."

I went out to tell the others what had happened and explained that they could see Bryce, but we needed to let him rest, and we shouldn't get him worked up. Pastor Susan came back first with Rob and me. The nurse was still trying to get Bryce's blood pressure down, so we said another prayer for Bryce before Susan said her goodbyes.

⊰◇⊱◇⊰◇⊱

The surgeon from the local children's hospital was helping the nurse look at Bryce's blood pressure. He told us, "Bryce's heart was so used to pumping against that leak so hard that it was trying to return to what it knows. It needs to get used to the new valve."

Two by two, the family came to see Bryce. It was hard for everyone to see our four-year-old little boy hooked up to so many wires and lying there as his body fought 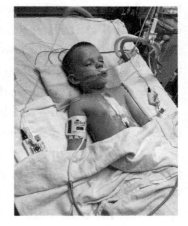 to get used to its new anatomy. Bryce had IVs in each hand and foot. The IV in his left hand was being used to take blood every so often to check his platelets because they had to give him pints of blood during surgery. He had a central line in his right hip, the wound drain tube below his ribcage, a blood pressure cuff on his right arm, a pulse ox on his right big toe, a ventilator in his mouth, and a urinary catheter.

When Dr. Stewart returned to check on Bryce again, his blood pressure was coming down, and the drainage started slowing down. Dr. Stewart was looking at the chest x-ray they had taken of Bryce after surgery, so Rob and I got to see it, too. I could see the wires they had used to bring his bones back together. They looked like tiny lassos around Bryce's little bones. Now that Bryce's blood pressure was coming down, and he was finally sleeping and resting peacefully, we decided to run to the cafeteria to eat dinner with the remaining visitors: Liza, my mom, and Jerry. I called Reyna, who was home with Aunt Cindy, to let her know that Bryce was doing okay.

She was glad to hear his surgery went well. She said, "The school guidance counselor came to talk to me today during school. She asked me if I was doing okay and asked if I wanted to talk about Bryce's surgery. She gave me a teddy bear wearing a school sweatshirt, and she gave me one to give to Bryce too!" Reyna couldn't wait to be able to visit Bryce and give him that bear.

After dinner, Rob and I headed back to the room to see how Bryce was doing. Everyone had gone home for the day except Liza, who stayed with us at the hospital. We talked to the nurse when we went back to Bryce's room. She was still monitoring his blood pressure and told us, "Bryce is somewhat coherent and starting to come out of anesthesia."

Liza was standing near the ventilator on Bryce's left side, and Rob and I were on the opposite side of the bed. As we were looking at him, Liza told the nurse, "I think he's choking."

I looked at Bryce and noticed he looked like he was pushing his tongue as if trying to get something out of his mouth ... the ventilator. The next thing I saw, Bryce had grabbed the ventilator and was trying to rip it out! Liza was so quick, caught Bryce's arm, and stopped him from pulling it out. Just then, blood started spraying everywhere. I couldn't see where it was coming from. Apparently, as Liza reached for Bryce's arm, she must have bumped his hand, and one of the IVs came out. It was the IV they were using to monitor his platelets.

Thankfully, the nurse said, "I can get blood from one of his other ports. I won't have to put it back in." Once again, God's grace was there for us at the precise moment we needed Him.

The next step was to wean Bryce off the ventilator, but they needed to get his blood pressure under control. They had restrained Bryce's hands now, and his arms were tied down. I hated seeing him like that, but I understood they didn't want to risk him trying to pull the ventilator out again. I asked the nurse, "What would have happened if Bryce had succeeded in pulling that out?"

"He would not have been awake enough to breathe on his own and his lung would have collapsed. Then we would have had to resuscitate him."

The nurse had seemed agitated when Liza knocked the IV out, but having heard what might have happened if Liza had not been there and reacted when she did, I was thankful that only an

IV collapsed and not Bryce's lungs. I thought, *I have no idea how they would have resuscitated a child who just had his chest wired back together. They wouldn't be able to push on his chest.*

I couldn't let my mind go any further. I don't even want to imagine what might have happened if Liza had not been watching him and standing so close when she stopped Bryce's hand.

While we were waiting in Bryce's room and watching him rest, the physician's assistant, who had been in surgery with Bryce, came to check on him. While she was there, she handed me a paper about the size of a business card. She told me, "It has an ID number on it that will identify where the valve came from and which donor. If you want to sign up to the organization listed on the card, it's voluntary for both parties so you may reach out, but that doesn't guarantee that you will hear from the donor family."

It was at this moment that it really hit home for me that Bryce had received an organ from another human being. I knew he was going to—the surgeons had told us it was a donor valve. But the reality of where it came from hit me like a huge weight in that moment as I stood next to my son's hospital bed, knowing that valve saved his life. It was then that I felt the gravity of the sacrifice another human being made to save the life of another. I tucked that piece of paper with the donor ID number tightly away with my important papers. I definitely wanted to reach out to the donor family ... even if it was only to express my sincere gratitude for their loving and selfless act of kindness.

Later that evening, it was nearly eight o'clock, and Bryce's blood pressure was finally under control. He was semi-coherent and starting to wake up, so the nurse started weaning him off the ventilator. I wasn't too sure how I felt about this. On the one hand, I wanted my son off that machine and breathing on his own. On the other, I felt we should let him sleep and not feel pain. Very quickly, it seemed, Bryce gave a big cough, and the nurse pulled the ventilator out. Shortly after, she had him out of that bed and sitting in a chair!

Bryce's first words were, "I'm so firsty."

He wanted a popsicle, but the nurse said he had to wait. She didn't want him throwing up, so she gave him a lemon sponge to swab his mouth. Bryce did not think that was an even trade and continued asking, "When can I have a popsicle?"

His mouth and lips were so dry. I remembered I had packed a ChapStick and asked the nurse if I could give it to him. She said, "As long as it is his and hasn't been used by someone else."

"It's brand new."

I was surprised ChapStick wasn't something the hospital had for patients. After Rob visited with Bryce for a while, we were going to let Bryce rest, so Rob went home to pick up Reyna. Bryce and I put the *Cars* movie on the television in his room, but I ended up watching it alone, holding Bryce's hand beside his bed while he slept. For the most part, the night was fairly peaceful, and Bryce was left to rest. The nurses kept a steady stream of pain meds flowing through his IV. I was grateful it allowed him to sleep. Tomorrow was going to be a busy day. The nurse already said, "We are getting him up and walking."

*I don't know if I'm ready for that.*

❖❖❖

The first day post-op was Friday, June 2nd, 2017. The same nurse from the previous day was back. She looked at Bryce and said, "Well, are you ready to get out of that bed?"

Bryce didn't even give it a second thought and was raring to go. I was staring at Bryce with all those wires and tubes still attached to him with a puzzled look. *How in the world is he going to walk with all that attached to him?*

The nurse must have read my mind as she turned to me and said, "We just grab all the wires and unplug the little portable monitor from the wall and we're off."

Sure enough ... she unplugged him, helped Bryce get out of bed, stood him up, and we went for a walk around the PICU floor. Bryce was doing great! As we walked, other nurses on the floor were cheering for him and telling him, "You are doing great!" They must have all known that he was a heart patient making his first round after surgery. It was so uplifting; my heart was filled with such joy. We turned the last leg of the floor; we only had one more left to make until we would be back to his room.

Suddenly, Bryce stopped and doubled over in pain. I thought the nurse had tugged on the wound drain hose by accident. Bryce would absolutely not budge and was crying in agony. I went straight over to him, picked him up from under his butt, and told the nurse, "He's done for now." I carried him back to his room and sat him on the bed. I was trying to comfort Bryce to get him to calm down so I could understand what was hurting him.

The nurse said, "It is probably gas. Often, heart patients say the gas pains hurt worse than the surgery." She explained, "When patients are on the bypass machine, it is only doing the work of your heart and lungs. All of your other organs shut down, and the stomach and intestines are one of the last organs to wake up. That's why we like to get them up and walking quickly after surgery to wake up those organs. I can give him a laxative, but since he hasn't had any food for two days, I don't think it will do anything for him."

A little while later, Liza came to the hospital. I was so thrilled to have some help because listening to Bryce cry out in pain was becoming increasingly overwhelming. I felt so incredibly helpless and was practically in tears when Liza arrived. It was the first time since we'd been at the hospital that Bryce showed signs he was in real pain, and I hated the fact that I couldn't do anything to help relieve his suffering. Bryce kept saying he wanted to go to the bathroom, so the nurse brought in a kid's size port-a-potty to sit on. He didn't go. She finally gave him some pain meds that helped Bryce relax, and we got him into bed to rest.

Rob and Reyna came to see Bryce around 5:30 that evening. Reyna was so happy to see Bryce, and she gave him the teddy bear the school counselor had given to her. Reyna sat next to Bryce on his bed and asked, "How are you feeling?"

She helped get him his drink or whatever he needed. The nurse had put a hospital shirt on Bryce so that Reyna couldn't see the incision or the wound drain. We didn't want her to be afraid or show fear that might cause Bryce to think there was a reason to be afraid. The nurse wanted to take Bryce for another walk.

"I'm not going," I told Rob. "Please, will you go with him this time? I can't take it if he cries out in pain the way he did earlier."

So Rob and Reyna took Bryce for a walk with the nurse. He cried and clung to Rob the entire way around. I could hear Bryce crying as he moved closer to the room. I stood in the doorway waiting as he made it all the way around this time, but he was not happy about it. Bryce's reward for walking the entire floor was all the popsicles he wanted. In fact, he ate so many popsicles they had to borrow some from another department because Bryce had eaten all the popsicles on the PICU floor!

The rest of the evening went fairly well, and Bryce was in good spirits and not really complaining of any pain. Later into the night, the pains started again. It was nearly midnight, and most of the kids on the floor were sleeping. Bryce was crying out in pain. I pressed the call button for his night nurse and told her, "His gas pains are back."

She helped get Bryce back on the port-a-potty and left to get something. It felt like she was gone forever. Bryce was sobbing and pleading for me to take him home. "Please!" he cried. "I just want to go home. I love to poop at home."

As we waited, I was doing my best to calm and console him. "I know, Bryce. I know you are hurting. She is coming back with something to help you."

He continued to cry out several more times, "Please! I wish she would hurry up!"

I tried to console him as we waited. "She's coming, honey. She went to get you some medicine to help stop the pain. You're being so strong, Bryce."

It was heart-wrenching, and I tried so hard to stay calm and keep myself from crying. Finally, the nurse came back. She gave him Tramadol, but she also gave him MiraLAX to help him pass the gas. After a little while, the pain meds kicked in, and we got Bryce to lie back down to sleep.

Four hours later, around four in the morning, I woke to the sounds of Bryce's laughter. Through exhausted eyes, I could see the silhouette of the nurse sitting beside him, and they were both giggling. Then I heard the loudest fart come from Bryce and realized what they had been giggling about.

I was so grateful to hear my son's laughter amid so much pain and recovery. *Finally! The gas bubbles were starting to move, and he was finally getting some relief! Why did we not give him the MiraLAX earlier? Thank God for sending us this night nurse to stop Bryce's agony.*

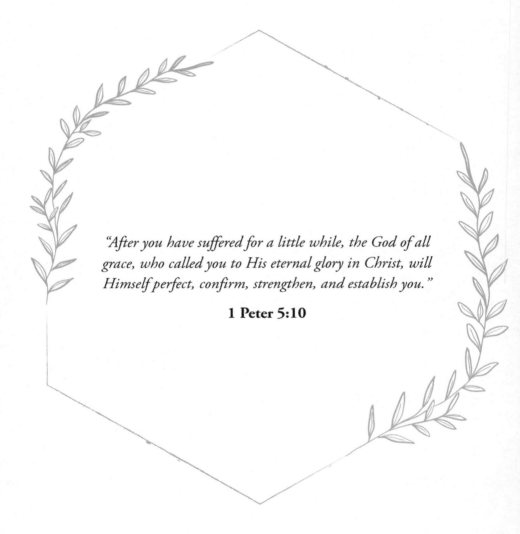

*"After you have suffered for a little while, the God of all grace, who called you to His eternal glory in Christ, will Himself perfect, confirm, strengthen, and establish you."*

**1 Peter 5:10**

# 23

# A Child's Resilience

Day three of our hospital stay proved to be a stepping stone to going home. Bryce was drinking more fluids, mostly from all the popsicles he was still devouring. He wasn't eating much in terms of solids yet, and his gas pains were not completely gone. We went for another walk around the PICU floor.

Bryce was fairly apprehensive. We made it the full way around this time without tears. When we got back, the nurse said, "The physician's assistant will be by to take out the drain tube today, and if Bryce continues doing well, you will likely move to the step-down floor."

"Will it be painful when they take out the drain tube?" I asked.

"It doesn't hurt, but it might feel weird to him because that tube is wrapped around his heart, and it might feel funny when they pull it out. We will give him some Tramadol in his IV before they take it out, which should help."

When the physician's assistant and the cardiologist on duty came to the room to take out the drain tube, I asked about the Tramadol. They said they thought the nurse put it in his IV. I turned on a movie for Bryce, thinking he could watch the television as a distraction.

Then the cardiologist laid Bryce's bed back so he couldn't see anything but them. One was on the right, and the other was on the left side of the bed. Bryce started screaming as he stared at the tube being pulled from his chest. It was so long that the cardiologist and the physician's assistant were taking turns hand over hand, pulling it out. I tried to divert Bryce's eyes to me, "Look at me, Bryce. Talk to Mama. Don't look at it. I'm right here."

They were still pulling the tube out. "It will be over soon, Bryce. You will feel better once it's out. Please, Bryce, look at Mommy." I could not break his gaze on that never-ending tube as he continued to scream the entire time it was being pulled from him. When they finally had the entire tube free from Bryce, he cried, and I did my best to hold him. I couldn't really hug him because of his incision, so I continued trying to console him. "I'm here. You're okay now. Look, that tube is all gone."

Bryce looked at me through tears and said, "Remember when you told me to look away when the lady took my blood because you said it wouldn't hurt as bad?"

"Yes, I remember."

"Well, I tried and tried to watch my movie, but they were in my way, and I couldn't see!" My heart nearly broke into pieces after hearing this.

"I know, Bryce. I'm sorry that hurt you. I didn't know it would. You were so brave and being so tough through everything."

When the nurse returned, I mentioned to her how awful Bryce had screamed when they took out the tube. She said, "They took it out already? I had not given him the Tramadol yet. I don't know why they didn't come get me."

*I knew it! I didn't think the nurse had given it to him, but they are putting so many different medicines in his IVs, I can't possibly know which one's he's getting.*

I was still very aggravated when Rob walked through the door a little later. I told him he had the worst timing. "Once again, I feel like I'm the bad guy because I was the one here when they ripped the tube out and hurt him."

Rob jokingly asked Bryce, "What did Mommy let them do to you?"

I shot him an incredulous look. "I am not in the mood for your jokes."

He started laughing, which made Bryce laugh.

"I still don't think you're funny." I gave a sigh of relief and laughed too. Thankfully, that part was over.

⋄⋄⋄⋄

As if someone flipped a light switch, Bryce was sitting up and feeling so much better. The nurse asked, "Do you want to try to walk the PICU floor again?"

Bryce was a little apprehensive at first. But once he realized how much better he felt without that drain tube, he was off and ready to run. He wanted to show Rob how he could walk the floor now. The nurse unhooked Bryce, gave Rob the portable monitor, and Bryce went for a walk with Rob and Reyna. I sat on the couch in the room to collect myself and thank God for helping us through that ordeal. I ended my prayer, *And thank You for sending Rob to lighten the mood when You did. I needed to laugh. Thank You, Jesus. You always know exactly what I need.*

While Rob and the kids were out for their walk, the nurse said, "They are preparing a room on the sixth floor for Bryce," so I started packing up all of our stuff and getting ready to move.

When Bryce returned, they helped him get into a wheelchair, and Reyna was already calling dibs that she wanted to push the wheelchair. Suddenly, I noticed a look of concern on Bryce's face. I figured he was not happy about Reyna pushing him in the chair. I kneeled down beside him and asked, "What's wrong, buddy?"

"I thought you said you were going to stay with me the whole time until I go home."

I reassured him, "I'm not going anywhere."

"Then why are you packing your stuff?" he innocently asked.

"I'm packing all of *our* stuff. Yours too. We are both going to a new room," I explained.

Bryce sat up and looked happy hearing this. "So you are staying with me until I go home?"

"Yes, just like I promised! I'm not going anywhere without you!"

Bryce was all smiles after that, and it didn't even bother him that Reyna was pushing him to the new room.

On the way to the step-down room, we passed by the playroom. As soon as Bryce took one look at it, he yelled, "Stop! I want to go to the playroom!"

The nurse let us stop and have a look and explained the rules: "You can take toys to your room to play with and if you play with anything, you must put it on the shelf to be cleaned."

We went to the new room and unpacked. Bryce asked me, "Mom, did you bring my clothes?"

"Yes, why?"

"I want to get dressed so I can play in the playroom."

Bryce didn't want to go there in hospital clothes. While Bryce was changing, a hospital volunteer dropped off a delivery for Bryce. It was a giant Lightning McQueen mylar balloon and some snacks from one of Bryce's friends at preschool. It made Bryce so happy to hear from his sweet friend.

Once he was dressed, Bryce started running down the hallway toward the playroom. He took off so fast I had not yet unplugged the portable monitor from the wall. The wires that were attached to the leads on his back yanked him backward, causing Bryce to slip in the hallway.

"You scared the daylights out of me!" I said to Bryce.

He shouted, "You hurt my back!"

"I didn't do it, Bryce. You didn't wait for me. The leads are stuck to your back, and they pulled on you when you went too far. You are not supposed to be running, anyway!"

I unplugged the monitor, and we walked carefully to the playroom. Bryce was thrilled to see they had a huge bucket of Legos. When Kearston and Rian came to see him, Bryce, his brother, and Rob built a huge tower with the Legos. Bryce had one of the button-up shirts I had brought from home, and with it buttoned, you couldn't see his scar. You would not know this child had just had heart surgery until you noticed the leads that peeked out from underneath the back of his shirt. Seeing him happily playing Legos with his dad and brother made me smile. Bryce seemed like his normal self. I nearly forgot we were sitting in a hospital playroom. Bryce loved the Legos so much that they let him take the whole box to his room.

Liza stopped by the hospital to visit that evening and then asked if Reyna wanted to come home with her so that Rob could stay and visit longer.

⧫⧫⧫

The next day, Sunday, Bryce discovered that they also had a Wii in the playroom and asked me to play "Big Bowser" with him. "Big Bowser" was what Bryce called the Super Mario game they had. After a while, the nurse stopped by to check on us, and Bryce looked at me and asked, "Can she play with me, Mom?"

"I guess if she has time, but I think she might be pretty busy."

The nurse said, "I can play with you for a little while."

Bryce told me to give her my controller because "You're not too good, Mom."

*Ha! Now I understand why he asked the nurse to play. Someone is feeling better, and that is enough for me.*

Later in the day, Bryce had several more visitors. Among them were his brother Rian, his sister Kearston, and Rian's fiancée, who all stopped by to see him again before Kearston had to catch her plane back home. We were struggling to get Bryce to eat anything. They were not going to release him to go home until he went to the bathroom, and he couldn't go to the bathroom if he didn't eat. He was still eating all the popsicles he wanted. In fact, he ate so many, the nurse finally showed me where to find the popsicles so I could go get them for Bryce myself. I warned her, "He already ate all the popsicles on the PICU floor, so you might want to call for reinforcements in case he eats all yours, too."

We tried all day to get Bryce to eat solid food. Only when Liza and Reyna showed up with pigs-in-a-blanket (tiny hotdogs wrapped in crescent rolls) and cookies they had made special for Bryce did he finally eat. It was the first solid food he had eaten since Wednesday night the week before. We were hoping this might mean Bryce could be released the next day.

On Monday, Rob had to go back to work, so my mom and Aunt Cindy came up to visit with Bryce after Reyna got on the bus for school. I confided to my mom, "I think I may have developed a urinary infection while I've been in here with Bryce. I haven't been drinking enough water. When we were in the PICU, I never wanted to miss the doctors doing rounds, so I was going too long without drinking anything. Then we moved to this floor, and we don't have a designated nurse assigned to Bryce the way he did in the PICU, so I haven't wanted to leave him alone to get anything for myself from the cafeteria."

I forgot to put on my own mask first. Sometimes we have to relearn the lessons the hard way. My mom said to call my doctor.

"No way. I'm not leaving the hospital. They may release him to go home today."

"Just call," she sternly said. "Explain what's going on, and see if he will just call in a prescription."

So I called my family doctor and explained the situation to the nurse who answered. I told her, "I know the symptoms because I've had one before, and I just need an antibiotic. I'm staying at the hospital with my four-year-old son, and I can't leave to go to a doctor's appointment."

Later that afternoon, my doctor called back, saying, "I will call in a prescription for you, but I want you to come into the office once you're back home so we can make sure the antibiotics worked."

My mom said, "I will pick up the prescription for you, so you won't have to stop on the way home and take Bryce into the store."

*I guess we all just need our moms sometimes, even when we're grown adults taking care of our own babies.*

After lunch, Bryce finally went to the bathroom. I never thought I would be celebrating my child using the bathroom, but there we were doing the potty dance because that meant we were going home! Rob came to the hospital after work and brought Reyna with him. The nurse helped load Bryce's gifts, balloons, and snacks into a little red wagon that Bryce got to ride out to the parking deck.

On the way home, we had to roll Bryce's favorite Simba blanket and place it between him and the seatbelt, so it didn't rub on his incision. When we arrived at home, Rob told Bryce, "Go inside and we will get all of your toys and gifts from the car." Bryce went into the house, or so we had thought. As we were unloading the car, Bryce decided he couldn't wait for his storm trooper, so he snuck out to the garage to get it from the car. Just as Rob started to tell Bryce he was told to stay in the house, Bryce slipped on the cement garage steps and fell, landing right on his chest. We had not been home for an hour, and Bryce had already fallen. I thought, *This is only the first day. Please God, help us get through these next six weeks!*

I was thrilled to be home and sleeping in our own beds again. Being home also meant the nurses weren't there to check on Bryce to make sure his blood pressure was okay or that his blood oxygen level was above 92. Now that we were home, pain monitoring became our responsibility. We were on a four-hour rotation between Motrin and Tylenol for the first couple of weeks. With each passing day, Bryce was feeling stronger. Keeping him from pushing his sternal limitations became increasingly difficult.

The first weekend we were home from the hospital, I walked out on the porch to find Bryce halfway up the rock-climbing wall of his playset. While running to get him, I shouted, "Bryce! You are not allowed to climb!"

I had to pick him up from under his butt and lift him off the playset as he wailed, "I can't even climb?"

He was also not supposed to play with Nerf guns or his play swords. Every time I turned around, I would see Bryce with another sword. "Where do you keep finding these things?" I asked him.

"I'm not telling you," he slyly answered. Meanwhile, the pile on top of the refrigerator was growing higher with every confiscation.

⋘⋙

The first Sunday we were home from the hospital, I had gone back to church. I wanted to tell everyone thank you for praying and keeping Bryce in their thoughts and to update them on how he was doing. Bryce didn't come with me, since we were trying to be cautious about any sickness or infections. After services, some of the women of the church gave me a huge bag of "surprises" for Bryce and Reyna. They had a gift for both kids for each day of Bryce's six-week sternal restriction. They had wrapped books, crayons, coloring books, bubbles, a bubble gun, puzzles, games, and so many other neat things to keep the kids occupied. I was blown away by our church family's generosity and thoughtfulness and was so grateful that they included Reyna as well. Every morning, Bryce would come downstairs and ask, "Can I open a prize?" It gave him something to look forward to every day, and each surprise helped to keep Bryce's busy hands occupied—at least for a little while.

By the week three post-op, I was telling the cardiologist that Bryce wasn't even asking for pain medicine, and I wasn't giving it to him unless he said he was uncomfortable. The cardiologist took the sutures off at this visit and said, "His scar is healing very well."

Bryce asked, "Can I swim in the pool?"

The doctor said, "It's okay if you want to float in the pool, but no aggressive movements and no raising your arms above your head."

Bryce was so excited to be allowed to swim in the pool, and Reyna was thrilled, too, because the only time she had been able to swim was when Bryce was taking a nap. The following weekend, we decided to go ahead and let Bryce float in the pool. He was doing fine at first and simply floating and taking it easy. Then, he must have gotten bored because the next thing I knew, Bryce was wiggling around and twisting his arms and body. I kept telling him to stop and reminding him what the doctor told him, "no aggressive arm movements." Finally, I had to make Bryce get out of the pool because he would not stop twisting and shaking his arms around.

That night, as I lay sleeping, I heard Bryce crying. I went to his bedside and asked, "What's wrong?"

He cried out, "Bees! Bees are stinging me!"

I frantically tried to focus my eyes to see the bees he said were in his room. Seeing none, I told him, "There are no bees in your room."

I realized it must have been his chest hurting from all the wiggling around in the pool that day. I ran to get the Motrin, but the pain was so intense Bryce could not sleep. It was the most pain and discomfort Bryce had felt since we came home from the hospital. Four hours later, Bryce was still crying out in pain, so I gave him Tylenol. "You should have listened to me in the pool. This is why you were told not to move your arms so much," I told him sternly.

"You were right, and I was wrong."

Boy, do I wish I had recorded him saying that! As much as I was irritated at him for not listening, I felt horrible that he was in so much pain. It took nearly twenty-four hours of rotating the Motrin and Tylenol before we finally got the pain under control. After that, we waited about a week to let Bryce try floating in the pool again.

⬦⬦⬦⬦

Of course, the unsolicited advice never stopped, and again, I found myself receiving guidance from people who had no idea what we were going through. One day when I was working from home, a lady from work messaged me asking an accounting question. "Are you in the office today?" she asked.

"I am working from home," I replied. "My son just had open heart surgery."

She then proceeded to tell me, "Whatever you do, don't let him play video games."

I stared at the screen. *What a presumptuous thing to say!*

We had set up Bryce's older brother's GameCube for him to play because it was one of the few things he would do and sit still. I didn't even respond to her comment about the video games, but simply answered her accounting question and then signed off. I have learned by now that people who have not walked in my shoes cannot relate and do not understand what six weeks of sternal restrictions with a rambunctious little boy is like. It's one thing to tell a mother you wouldn't suggest allowing your kids to play video games if your child was afforded the opportunity to run, play outside, climb a playset, swing a bat (or a play sword), throw a ball, or ride a bike. My child couldn't do any of these things. I was not about to listen to this misguided advice. I understood this now, though the words still stung. I was getting better at ignoring it and letting it roll off my back. Allowing it to upset me didn't hurt anyone but myself.

In the pre-Covid world, telling people you were not going to watch fireworks because you didn't want to risk your child getting sick from taking him in public usually was followed with a question of, "Why not?"

I explained this to several family and friends when we declined an offer to watch fireworks with them. "It's not worth the risk," I told them. Bryce had heard me say multiple times that we couldn't take him out in public. This came back to bite me around the six-week mark of Bryce's sternal restrictions. I was experiencing what you might refer to as "cabin fever." We had been home the entire summer, and except for doctor visits and the few times I had returned to the office, we had not been anywhere. Bryce was also getting more energetic by the day as his bones were now nearly healed, and with that new valve, he was feeling pretty spunky.

I told the kids, "Get your shoes on. We are going out for lunch."

There was a small café down the road from our house. We were going at an odd time, so we would miss the lunch rush, but I needed to get out of the house. Bryce's next heart appointment was coming up, and I fully expected them to release him of his restrictions. We had a nice lunch, and I felt better having a chance to talk to someone over the age of eight.

As we left the café and I was putting Bryce in his car seat, he asked me, "Do I still have to take a nap when we get home?"

"Yes."

Bryce got quiet for a minute and then said, "Well, the next time I go to my heart doctor appointment, I'm going to tell him you took me out in public!"

I laughed quietly to myself the whole way home and thought, *I am blessed to have this spirited, resilient little kid to keep me on my toes, and I am blessed to be the one he calls "Mom."*

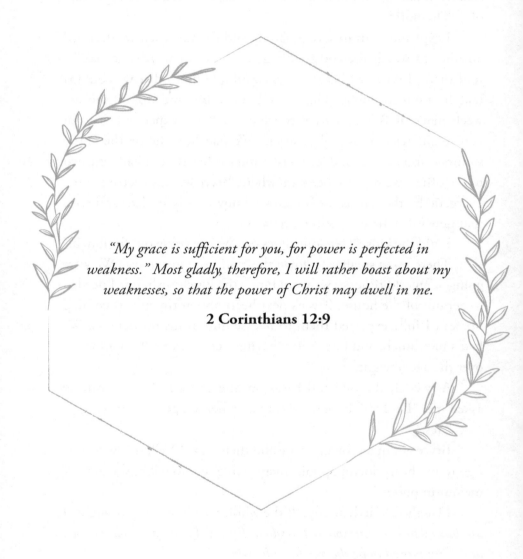

*"My grace is sufficient for you, for power is perfected in weakness." Most gladly, therefore, I will rather boast about my weaknesses, so that the power of Christ may dwell in me.*

**2 Corinthians 12:9**

# 24

# Finding Forgiveness

As I waited for services to begin, I read the passage of Scripture in the church bulletin and struggled to understand it. *What does this mean, "my grace is sufficient for you"?* I was about to learn the lesson that would break me free of years of self-blame, guilt, resentment, and anger. This Scripture is part of a gospel lesson where the apostle Paul asked the Lord three times to remove a thorn in his flesh, which he said had come from the messenger of Satan (verses 7–8). The Lord responded to Paul's request by telling him, "My grace is sufficient for thee."

Our church pastor explained, "God could have removed the thorn and healed Paul; instead, He used the infirmity to humble him. While God did not cause Paul's suffering, the thorn in his flesh served as a reminder that Paul should not praise himself, boast or become conceited."

Pastor Susan helped open my eyes to understand the thorn in my own flesh. For nearly two and a half years after Bryce's birth, I carried such a heavy burden on my heart, and I prayed every night, asking God to place His healing hands on my son to take away this affliction from Bryce and heal his valve. I blamed myself that my son was born with a congenital heart disease (CHD). I replayed my entire pregnancy over and over, trying to pinpoint what I did to cause Bryce to live a life full of heart surgeries. I was carrying so much guilt for working 60- to-70-hour weeks, not permitting myself the proper rest a mother with a child required; and carrying the tremendous weight I felt for not advocating stronger when Bryce was in heart failure.

Although the doctors had all said it wasn't anything I or anyone else did, I felt like God had used Bryce to teach me a lesson; to make me realize what was truly important in life. I felt it was my fault that my son had to face such difficult obstacles in his young life. Reading God's Word and hearing that He would not inflict pain on someone to teach us His grace had given me peace. I was finally able to understand that God doesn't cause bad things to happen; He uses the circumstances to bring forth blessings, new beginnings and lessons to keep us humble. In my pastor's words, "We are never the same people after experiencing the thorns and we have a choice of becoming more faithful and finding the blessings or becoming bitter or more fearful."

I knew I was not the same person I was when we started this roller coaster ride that has been Bryce's CHD journey, and yes; I think God had used this experience to teach me a valuable lesson about what truly is important in life: God, faith, and family. I know that the entire experience has strengthened my faith and brought me closer to God than ever before in my life. I would not be here writing this book if it were not for all the lessons God has helped me to understand throughout this entire experience.

I will not pretend that the moment I heard this sermon and understood the lesson from the apostle Paul, I could immediately forgive myself. Forgiveness is a journey in itself and can be a daily struggle. After learning to look at our situation through a different lens, I was able to change my perspective, and my eyes no longer saw the obstacles. Instead, I looked for the blessings. When my son needed open heart surgery, I wrote a letter to God thanking him for all the blessings He had bestowed upon us:

*Father in Heaven,*

*I thank You for giving us the blessings we have been given: access to skilled medical physicians, surgeons, and hospitals so close to our home so our family does not have to be separated again, access to health care insurance to help us afford the cost of the surgery and hospital stay, the valve donor who gave their organs following a terrible tragedy that they may have endured, which ended their life, but gave my son a new beginning to his.*

*I am grateful to have a huge support system in both our family and friends; I'm thankful my mom is retired, healthy, and willing to help us with getting Reyna to school while Bryce is having surgery and in recovery, and also for her willingness to help watch Bryce when I have to return to work. I am grateful to have my husband by my side through this journey. I am especially grateful for advancements in medical technology so that Bryce doesn't have to get a metal valve and the replacement valve will not have to be open heart surgery.*

*I am thankful for the many doctors, scientists, engineers and funding that is put towards learning more and leading to further medical enhancements of quality of life and life-expectancy for kids born with a CHD. I am thankful to work for a company and a boss that affords me the benefit of working from home while I care for Bryce so that our household income is not detrimentally affected when we need it to pay the costs of his surgery. I am grateful for the FMLA laws that protect my job and benefits so I can take care of my child. I'm grateful that the daycare is not going to force me to pay to hold Bryce's spot in the Frog Room, while he's out for six weeks. And finally, I am grateful to have God on our side to carry my son through this journey.*

In the fall of 2017, following Bryce's open heart surgery and after he was released from sternal restrictions, I decided I was finally ready to reach out to the donor family. I searched through the important papers I had brought home from the hospital. I could not find it. I began pulling papers out of the desk, shuffling them from the pile on the counter. "Where is it?" I shouted, not really talking to anyone in particular. "What did I do with that thing?"

"What are you looking for?" Rob asked.

"I'm looking for that piece of paper the physician's assistant gave me. It looks kind of like a business card, but it's thinner paper." I picked up the journal I had taken to the hospital and flipped through the pages. "Thank God! Here it is!" I shouted.

"What are you going to do with it?"

"I'm going to register Bryce's valve implant to this CryoLife site with the ID number she gave us."

Rob asked if they would tell us who the donor family was. I reminded him, "No. The physician's assistant said it was all completely voluntary ... for both parties. Even if we register, it doesn't mean they will agree to reach out to us. I want to sign up to see if I can at least write to them."

Within a few days of registering, I received an email from Allison Rickman, thanking me for registering on CaringtoShare.org. Allison explained, "You can write a letter to the donor family and send it to me. I will forward it along to the donor family. You can send photos, but no contact information at this time."

I thanked her for her help and told her I would finish the letter and send it to her. She emailed back and asked, "Did Bryce's surgeon tell you anything about the donor? I am allowed to share the age, gender, and state the donor resided in, if you would like to know."

I responded and told her, "The surgeon didn't give us anything further than the card to register. My husband and I would like to know this information, if you could share it with us."

Four days later, I received her reply. "The donor was a four-year-old female from Michigan."

I was stunned. "A four-year-old?"

I called Rob and told him. He had the same response. "I just thought since the valve Bryce received was larger than the one he had replaced, that it came from someone older."

"I know. I did, too," I said. "My heart is aching for the family. Now I really want to write them a letter. I want to let them know that their decision helped to save our son," I finished as we hung up the phone.

It took me several weeks to finalize my letter to the donor family. I was wrestling with what is called "survivor's guilt." I didn't know the extent of the circumstances of why the donor family lost their child, but I knew that a parent or parents had to make the difficult decision and say yes to organ donation amid their own tragedy and loss. I wanted them to know that their decision was not in vain.

I wrote to the donor family, telling them about Bryce's CHD journey. I shared, "Bryce's energy and resilience have been remarkable. For the first time in my son's life, I have a very different picture of his long-term future and genuine hope that I will see him grow into adulthood. When Bryce was an infant, we were told that our son would never play coached sports. Following our son's valve replacement surgery, we were told that if Bryce would like to try sports, we can allow him, but we must respect him when he says he is tired or needs a break. These are doors and opportunities I didn't think would grace my son's life, and now it seems the world is his playground. For this, I thank you and your family for the gift of life that your dear loved one has bestowed on my son."

I finished my letter, "I realize this has to be a very hard thing to endure in the face of the tragedy of losing your loved one. I pray that you have found some sense of solace in hearing how much this unselfish act and gift to humanity has helped to heal another child."

Forgiveness for myself and letting go of the survivor's guilt were steps in the right direction, and this was helping me heal.

⋄⋄⋄⋄

**I** felt God telling me there was someone else I needed to forgive. I knew in my heart, but it took me a little longer to let go of the anger and resentment I had built up toward the pediatrician who initially missed the signs of heart failure when my son was an infant. I was being a hypocrite if I truly had given my heart to Christ. How could I be redeemed by the blood of Jesus, who died for my sins, if I cannot forgive others as He taught us? As it says in Ephesians 4:31–32:

> "All bitterness, wrath, anger, clamour, and slander must be removed from you, along with all malice. Be kind to one another, compassionate, forgiving each another, just as God in Christ also has forgiven you."

I made it a daily mission to ask God in prayer to help me let go of the anger and resentment toward the pediatrician, to fully forgive him. In time, I was able to do just that and I hold no ill-will or blame against him. Laying that anger down and releasing the pediatrician from the blame I had placed at his feet freed me of such an enormous weight that I had been carrying. Letting go of the bitterness eating away at my soul helped me forgive and heal. I was able to see that there were so many things during that time that either of us could have done differently to change the outcome of Bryce ending up with a 12 percent heart function.

The pediatrician had told me, "Bryce and one other child are the only two heart patients I have ever treated." I should have asked for a referral to another pediatrician with experience with CHD babies. Likewise, the pediatrician should have referred me to a colleague, or he should have called the cardiologist and kept him updated on Bryce's status. I also know that none of that would have altered Bryce going into heart failure. He would have still been in heart failure, but if we had noticed the signs earlier, we could have prevented the emergency surgery, the dilation of Bryce's heart, and the three days Bryce lived on a ventilator as his heart recovered.

I have accepted that this lesson has opened the door for me to share my testimony of faith with others. I pray it will help others learn from our experience and possibly prevent this from happening to another family. I truly believe that God also used this tragedy to put me on the path where I am today to share my testimony of faith so others can look for the blessings in their own life and witness God working for them every day.

# PART FOUR

# Trusting God

*"For by grace you have been saved through faith;
and this is not of yourselves, it is the gift of God;
not a result of works, so that no one may boast."*

**Ephesians 2:8–9**

# Having Faith

**B**ryce continued to thrive following his open heart surgery in June 2017. In fact, he grew two inches by August that year, and his energy level surpassed us all. The following summer, Bryce played baseball for the first time and loved it. I was not there to see when he first stepped onto that baseball field and had to live vicariously through pictures Rob sent me while I was at work.

In February 2018, I was appointed to a design team for a new system implementation at work. I was initially only assigned to the design team, which was supposed to be a six-month assignment. I agreed to be on the team with the stipulation that the project would not consume my life.

Before the kickoff meeting in March 2018, the design teams' location was changed. Instead of my normal commute, I would be in the car three hours a day (an hour and a half drive one way). The design team had more people than chairs available around the conference table, which meant it was first come, first serve for a seat. Since I had school-age children to drop off and a long commute, I was always one of the last people to arrive in the morning. This left me and four other team members sitting on plastic armless chairs with our laptops on our laps all day. The others sitting in the plastic chairs at the back of the room with me had to share the electrical outlet nearby to take turns charging our laptops.

As the design team wrapped up, it became very clear that there were not enough people to support the core team, which was supposed to help with the implementation scheduled for the first quarter of 2019. The project team asked my manager if I could remain on the core team, and he agreed with the condition that I could work from the office closer to my home. The design team turned into the core team, then the implementation team, the go-live, and finally, the go-live support team.

The core project team proved to be more intense than the design phase. I would work ten- and twelve-hour days, then commute back home. I often came home and logged back onto my laptop after my kids went to bed. The team was under so much pressure to hit the original go-live deadline; everyone was working nights, weekends and continuing to accumulate unused vacation time. There was so much to do and not enough time or people. The go-live date was changed two more times, but the team leads never took their foot off the pedal.

So much for not consuming my life. It was the hardest I have ever worked and the most intense pressure I've ever experienced in my entire career.

⋙⬦⬦⬦⬥⋘

Once again, I felt that tug that I was not living the life I was meant to live. This feeling was exacerbated by the letter we received from the school nurse in the fall of 2018. The kindergarten class had been given hearing tests. Bryce failed the test … in both ears. *How could I not have noticed that my child could not hear? I knew that he asked*

*"What?" a lot when I told him to do something, but I had chalked that up to selective hearing.* The test result showed red across the board. Red at every decibel. Another gut punch and example of me allowing work to overshadow my life.

I made an appointment with Bryce's ENT that November. The results showed that Bryce's hearing was below normal due to the holes from the tubes that had fallen out, but the holes never closed. The options presented to us were hearing aids or surgery.

"Hearing aids or put him through another surgery! I could just cry!" I told Rob. "I am not making this kid wear hearing aids! He already has to wear glasses, and he's self-conscious about his scar. I'm not giving kids one more thing to pick on him about!"

I scheduled an appointment in December with Dr. Nelson, the otolaryngologist, to see what would be involved in fixing the holes in Bryce's eardrums. Dr. Nelson's recommendation was, "Tympanoplasty to patch the holes from the ear tubes. Bryce's holes are too large to do a simple patch where I can overlay the holes with a small patch. Instead," he continued, "I will have to raise the layer of Bryce's outer eardrum and place the patch beneath it using a graft from his tragus. It should be an outpatient surgery, although Bryce's heart team may want him to stay overnight for monitoring."

The icing on the cake: "It will require two separate surgeries. We cannot do both ears on the same day because if I fix one side and lay Bryce on his other side, gravity will pull all my work right back out. I need the eardrum to set in place and have time to heal."

The first available date they could get Bryce scheduled was in seven months. We would have to wait until the following summer for Bryce even to get one of his ears fixed. Dr. Nelson said, "Bryce will have six weeks of restrictions following each surgery. Two weeks of physical activity limitations (no running, climbing, or Taekwondo), and an additional four weeks of swimming restrictions."

*Another summer of restrictions for Bryce.*

The second surgery was scheduled three months after his first one, which would be in October. They wanted to get it on the calendar so we wouldn't have to wait as long for the second surgery. *Seven more months Bryce will go without hearing properly.*

They were already starting to read in kindergarten, so it had already started affecting his ability to hear sounds correctly to read. One of my friends recommended, "You should reach out to the principal and get Bryce on a 504 plan, so they will make accommodations in the classroom for him."

I had never heard of a 504 plan and was so grateful to my friend for her suggestion. The principal at Bryce's school acted swiftly, and his teacher started using a microphone attached to a speaker at the back of the room.

On July 19th, 2019, two weeks after the final go-live date, Bryce had tympanoplasty surgery on his left ear. Overall, the surgery went well. He came home with a headband wrapped around his head, and on one side contained a hard plastic cover the size of half of a softball. He only had to leave the headband on at night to sleep. The cover was to prevent Bryce from rubbing his ear and deter him from lying on that side. After a few days of cycling Tylenol and Motrin, the only complaints came at bedtime when he had to wear the protective cover.

Rob and I planned to take the kids to Myrtle Beach on vacation after Bryce's ear had healed and he was released to swim again. After three days in South Carolina, Hurricane Dorian caused us to reroute our plans. We did not let this obstacle deter our time together. Instead, we finished the duration of our vacation in Tennessee, where our entire family went ziplining through scenic views of the Smokey Mountains.

A week later, Bryce tested for his purple belt in Taekwondo. I was so proud of him, and my heart was full of gratitude for his instructors, who worked with us to get Bryce to this milestone. Aside from 2018, Bryce has had surgery every year since he started Taekwondo at three years old. While he had to take several months or weeks off to recover over the last three and a half years, he always wanted to go back and keep trying to earn his next belt. I was glad to be able to be there to watch him test and earn it.

The second tympanoplasty surgery was scheduled for Wednesday, October 23rd, 2019. The surgeon said, "Things went well, and I was able to take a look at Bryce's left ear while we had him in there, and it is fully intact and looks great."

This surgery was a little different from our first time around. Bryce was much more uncomfortable and in pain. He also complained that the room was spinning, and he was sick to his stomach. They told us nausea and dizziness were both normal with this type of ear surgery because his equilibrium would need to adjust. Bryce had a harder time sleeping at night because the headband with the plastic cover prevented him from sleeping on his right side. We had to keep a diligent watch on the pain medication to ensure we didn't miss a rotation because his pain was much more severe with this surgery.

⬦⬦⬦

After finishing my time on the go-live support team, I returned to my prior role in operations. In the spring of 2020, my manager asked if I would be interested in returning to a business partnering role. I was still recovering from being on the I.S. project and didn't want to make the move. However, with the re-organization that had been going on, I felt that if I didn't apply for the open role, I might not have a job. I met with the GM of the business and some of his direct reports. The GM seemed like a down-to-earth kind of guy, and his direct reports had nothing but great things to say about him.

I agreed to apply to the business partnering role and was offered the senior position. I would be starting the new role in July 2020, when our entire office was working from home. This meant I would be transitioning remotely, meeting a new team remotely, and it would be during a quarter close and the start of strategic planning, which is one of the busiest times for a business finance partner.

About a month into the role, I started noticing red blotches on my left side. They itched at first and then moved around the side of my back and became painful. I scheduled an appointment with my family doctor, and my fears were confirmed … shingles. "I have shingles? I am only forty-seven years old! How in the world can I have shingles?" I asked my doctor.

He asked me if I had been under any stress. *Well, where should I start?* I thought. *I am fresh off an I.S. project that consumed eighteen months of my life, my son just had his second ear surgery, making it his ninth procedure in six years, I've been trying to be a mom and teacher to my kids while working from home since March 2020, and I just took a new job I'm learning remotely.* "Yeah, I'd say I'm under some stress," I told him.

The following month, while on a camping trip with my family, I received a call from my new manager. His message said, "I don't want to bother you, but I wanted to give you a heads-up about something so you won't worry."

I called him back, and he told me, "The GM for the business you are supporting took another role in a different segment, and you will be getting a new general manager. I don't want you to stress over it. I will help you manage through if needed."

*I should have listened to my body telling me to alleviate stress in my life.*

The new GM was more demanding. The first fourteen months of working together were challenging but manageable. Then, in the fall of 2021, there was a change in organizational leadership. Things shifted into high speed very quickly. I was back to working 70+ hour weeks. I worked nights, weekends and lost three days' vacation because there was never any time to take a break. Requests from the new administration came left and right and always with a tight turnaround.

I dipped into the arsenal of things I had learned about, focusing on what I could control and setting healthy boundaries, but those walls were bulldozed by demands sent at four in the morning with the expectation of a response by 8:00. Those healthy boundaries were met with indifference to the fact that I have a family or life outside of work. Still, the messages would scream through my phone during my daughter's volleyball game at eight o'clock at night, to which I would no longer be able to enjoy because my mind was now on the demand I would have to address when I got home.

After attending the local high school football game, Rob woke up Saturday, September 18, 2021, shivering and running a high fever. No one else was presenting any symptoms, and we had not been around anyone recently who had Covid, though I suspected that was what we were facing. I ordered several at-home tests, and my theory was confirmed: positive for Covid.

Two days later, I found Reyna taking her temperature and telling me her stomach hurt. As many families did during that time, we quarantined part of the family in one area of the house and did our best to keep the rest of the family healthy.

One week after Rob had presented symptoms, I lost my taste and smell. A test confirmed I now had it too. We were still doing everything we could to keep Bryce protected—concerned about how it would affect his heart. He basically had the entire top floor of the house to himself. At first, my symptoms were not bad. I mainly had a sinus headache and felt nauseous.

During the second week of my symptoms, I took a turn for the worse. My lungs were congested. I was having difficulty completing simple tasks. Walking to the bathroom or going upstairs would send me into a severe coughing bout. The virus had turned into pneumonia. Rob was still fighting extremely high fevers every day. With both of us fighting the virus, we could no longer prevent the one thing I had been dreading … Bryce began having symptoms.

I was struggling. On one hand, I was doing everything I could to care for my family and on the other, I was fighting to survive. I was on my second round of Azithromycin (an antibiotic), a cough suppressant, and was using an albuterol inhaler. My doctor had ordered budesonide and albuterol to use with a nebulizer three times a day to help clear my lungs so I could breathe. He also had me on Dexamethason (a steroid to prevent inflammation) and Zofran to help with nausea.

On the evening of October 1st, 2021, I suffered a coughing attack after taking my dog outside. When I went back into the house, I was still coughing and choking. I could not catch my breath. I tried to use the inhaler, but nothing was helping. I tested my blood oxygen levels with the pulse ox tester we had for Bryce. "My O2 is at 70 now," I told Rob.

I looked up and saw my daughter Reyna standing on the staircase, staring at me. She was frozen in fear as I struggled to catch my breath and get my coughing under control. "I will be okay, Reyna," I tried to comfort her.

She started sobbing and darted up the steps in tears. After a breathing treatment helped tame my coughing, I went upstairs to talk to Reyna. She was in my room when I found her. Looking up at me with tears streaming down her face, she said, "I don't want you to die, Mom."

I sat on the bed next to her and hugged her. "I'm not going to die, Reyna. I have so much faith! God will help us through this!"

Reyna asked if she could sleep in my bed that night, and I fell asleep holding her hand. My breath was so weak at that point. Each breath felt like minute gasps of air. As I closed my eyes to sleep that night, I prayed, *Father in Heaven, please heal my body with the blood of Jesus. I know You have the power to take this from me, Lord. Please let this be gone from me. I pray You will open my eyes in the morning and allow me to see my children's faces. I'm not ready to leave them, Father. I pray it is not yet my time.*

Rob returned to work on October 4th, 2021, having tested negative and no longer presenting any symptoms. Reyna had returned to school. Bryce had recovered but still had to quarantine for ten days. My dad, David, texted me. "How are you feeling?"

"My O2 levels were running at 70 over the weekend."

"Send me a picture of the pulse ox reading," he asked.

The pulse ox read: O2 75 and BPM 91. "The labels are wrong. That must be your pulse," he replied.

"The pulse is 91," I responded.

"That can't be right."

"It got pretty scary here the other night."

"Why didn't you call me? You know I have oxygen here. I could have helped you!" he persisted. My dad has been on oxygen since 2009 after a fight with lung cancer.

"I've been using the inhaler, and the breathing treatments are beginning to help."

"Have Rob stop by here later and pick up one of my travel tanks. I'll have it ready! Tell him to come get it!" he insisted.

Later that day, while sitting on the picnic table waiting for my dog outside, I turned my head to gaze at the clear blue sky above me and began to pray. *Father in Heaven, we need You. I need You. Thank*

*You for healing Reyna and Bryce. I am grateful neither of them had symptoms longer than three days, and all of their symptoms were minor. Thank You for healing my husband and freeing him from the grip of the fever that plagued his body for fifteen days. Please, Father, heal me from this burden. Please cast this sickness out. It has become too heavy for me. I cannot carry it anymore. Please send your healing angels from heaven above to take this from me! In Jesus' name. Amen.*

After work, Rob stopped by my dad's, who showed him how to set up the oxygen tank and gave him one of his air hoses for me to use. Dad texted that evening asking for an update on my O2 levels. "I am at 88 now while using the oxygen."

"What is the reading on the oxygen tank?" he asked.

"Rob said it is in the red."

"I'm filling two tanks now and bringing them to you."

"You don't have to do that. I'm already starting to feel better. I was able to walk to the bathroom this evening without having a coughing fit. It's getting late, and I worry about you getting this," I persisted.

"Oh, I'm coming! I want to see your O2 levels for myself," he declared.

I knew I would not win this battle.

Dad knocked on my door with two newly filled oxygen tanks at 11:00 that night. Rob answered the door, as I was still so worried about putting my dad at risk. For the next couple of days, my dad continued refilling his oxygen tanks, which were helping me fight to breathe. He told me later that he saw death in my eyes the night he brought the oxygen tanks to me. Eight days later, I slept lying down in my own bed, without being propped up by a wedge pillow, and free from coughing attacks. My O2 levels had finally returned to a normal level of 95 without oxygen.

Three days after professing my faith to my daughter, and placing all my faith at God's feet, He answered my prayers. He sent His healing angels through my dad and husband. While I still had a long way back to doing simple tasks without losing my breath, I was on the road to recovery, and my faith in God was stronger than ever. I returned to work on October 11th with direction from the on-site nurse that I would work from home as I regained my strength and continued healing.

*"This is My commandment, that you love one another, just as I have loved you."*

**John 15:12**

# 26

# Sometimes You Have to Walk Away

The businesses were asked to put together a new summarized version of the strategic plans we had recently completed. We were asked to include market and historical information about each business to help bring the new CEO up to speed. I was part of a smaller team within the business, working on the revised strategy update. I had been asked to update the financial trajectory based on very specific parameters provided by the GM. Again, we were under an extremely tight turnaround, and this update happened to coincide with the annual planning that was also ongoing. In addition, I was still recovering from pneumonia in early October. I was still on breathing treatments and was supposed to be getting my rest.

The updated trajectory was due on the same day budgets were scheduled to close in the system. I knew I would only meet the budget deadline if I stayed up all night finalizing the trajectory. I finished at 4:00 a.m., got up at 6:00 to take the kids to school, and called into the meeting the GM scheduled at 8:00 to talk through what was still needed to finalize the strategy presentation for the new CEO. When asked if the trajectory was finalized, I told him, "Yes, it is."

Sometime during the meeting, the GM said, "I need you to send me a spending trend for the last two years, the current year forecast, and next year's budget."

I tried to explain, "The budget deadline is actually today, and I won't be able to get that information until next week because everyone is still entering the cost budgets into the system, which is due by the end of the day. I am actually behind on our budgets and need to spend today getting that done."

The GM took off his glasses, rubbed his forehead, and as he began waving his arms in the air, he shouted, "Tracy, you need to help!" His words hit me like I had just been punched in the chest.

*I need to help? What does he think I've been doing all night?* I took a couple of breaths and tried to calm myself. I was so extremely tired from the lack of sleep, and his words stung. I had been helping him all night! I gave up my sleep to help him! I wanted to quit on the spot, but I wouldn't give him any satisfaction of having broken my spirit. I didn't say another word for the rest of the meeting. When he asked, "Does everyone know what you are supposed to do?"

I simply said, "Yep," and then turned off my camera and signed out of the video conference.

I emailed my boss and told him what had happened. "I cannot continue working like this," I told him. My manager called me later that morning to talk me out of quitting and told me he would remind the GM that he needed to be cognizant that I was still healing and needed my rest.

In the meantime, I called the finance analyst who reported to me and told her about the GM's request. As usual, she was willing to jump in and take a shot at the spending trend and would try to piece together the budget info for next year using what she could pull from the system and estimates for what we didn't have yet. This analyst was truly a godsend. I was just keeping my head above water with her help; I would have been drowning without her.

God must have known I would need a strong, highly competent person as my analyst during this season of my life, and He sent me one of the most efficient working people I've ever met. All I had to do was explain what I was looking for or needed, and she'd say, "Give me a bit, and I'll see what I can do." Within an hour, I would usually have either a draft or the final version of what I needed.

After we finished round two of the strategy update and had already finalized and presented the annual business plan to the segment VP of finance and the segment VP, we were told that the new administration wanted an altogether different set of budget slides. These would be reviewed with the new CEO. The GMs were supposed to submit their final budget files to the segment VP on Friday, December 10th, 2021. It was early December, and I had finished updating all the budget slides for the new template. I sent the completed file to the business GM for his review in advance of the requested deadline. On Tuesday morning, the week of the budget deadline, I received an email with a screen print of changes to the key initiatives that I had drafted in the budget file. I updated the file with the requested changes and sent the revised file the following day, Wednesday, December 8th.

Wednesday afternoon, I got a call from the school nurse saying, "Bryce is complaining of a stomachache. Something is going around. Could you come pick him up?" Bryce's stomach pains became increasingly worse throughout the next day. I was beginning to worry that he may have appendicitis because all the symptoms were the same as I had experienced in 2016 when I had an emergency appendectomy. I took him to the ER for evaluation. They took an ultrasound of his appendix, but it was inconclusive, so they monitored him for a few hours and sent us back home. They told us to come back if it got worse.

On Friday, I kept Bryce home from school, and his symptoms worsened to the point he asked me to take him back to the hospital. I had not seen that the GM had submitted the final budget package that was due. Before leaving for the hospital, I emailed my manager and forwarded the version I had sent to the GM on Wednesday. I told my manager, "In case you have not received the final budget package, I'm forwarding this to you so that you have it for the segment roll-up needed for Monday."

I took Bryce back to the ER that evening, after I worked a full day. I packed my work laptop to take with me. Bryce ended up being admitted to the hospital that night. They ran blood tests and checked him for Covid, the flu, and multiple other things. They ended up doing a CT scan to confirm that his appendix was not inflamed. It wasn't. Given his heart condition, they wanted to monitor his fluid intake and run a stool sample to do more tests.

Bryce remained in the hospital for the next two days with continued intestinal pain. In between tending to Bryce, I worked on updating a price-cost presentation for a meeting the GM had scheduled for Monday morning. Sunday, the tending physician came to see Bryce and told us they were able to pinpoint the virus from the results of his stool sample test. The virus had cleared Bryce's system, but it had caused mesenteric adenitis, which is the source of his stomach cramps, and it could take up to six weeks for the cramping to clear up. Sunday afternoon, Bryce was released from the hospital to go home.

The following morning, Monday, December 13th, I received the first response to the budget slides I had sent to the GM six days prior. "Why didn't you include the slide I already sent to you per the attached email? Please get that slide into the final deck for the CEO."

He had attached an email from two weeks prior in which he had changed some comments I had initially drafted. I reviewed the email he had attached and realized my mistake. When I read his comments previously, I didn't catch that he had changed anything, as his changes were minor. I forwarded an updated version to my manager, explaining my oversight, and asked if he would update our slides before he sent the consolidated segment.

I also vented my frustration to my manager, "I will admit my mistake. It was an oversight after so many iterations; however, I think this is ridiculous! I sent the updated budget template for his review the first week of December and received no response. Then, I received a screen print of changes on Tuesday morning, Dec 7th, with no mention that any previous changes were missing from the slide deck. I sent the final revised file on Wednesday, Dec 8th, and he didn't look at it until six days later! Then he proceeded to scold me for not including comments from changes he made two weeks ago! I spent all weekend in the hospital with my son and took my laptop with me to work on the information for the price-cost meeting he scheduled for this morning, and he can't take the time to review the slides I sent him last Wednesday? I am really growing tired of working like this."

This was what finally woke me up to let me know I needed a change. I knew I was fed up with feeling like I was chained to my laptop twenty-four-seven, but it wasn't until my eight-year-old son began asking me, on almost a daily basis, "When are you going to get a new job, Mom?" before I finally realized I was not on the path God meant for me. This was when I learned that when we take a path that does not lead to the road God intended for us, it will show up in ways we never expected until we finally wake up and see it for ourselves. Sometimes, it may take reaching a point where you absolutely cannot take it anymore before realizing this is not the purpose for your life. For me, God had an eight-year-old boy hold a mirror to my face for me to see that I was on the wrong path.

⬦⬦⬦⬦

In the winter of 2021, I updated my resume and started interviewing externally. I knew I had to get out of the toxic environment I was in, and although I had hoped to find something internally, I was willing to look elsewhere if that was what it took to find the work-life balance I needed for the sake of my family and my own health. In February 2022, an internal role was posted that piqued my interest. The director the role supported was a man of faith. I had worked with him on a project in the past. I knew he showed empathy for his direct reports and had compassion and understanding. The hiring manager was my former supervisor who had fought for me to work closer to home while on the core team of the new system implementation in 2018.

I applied and earned the new role. This time, I felt I was in a much better place and felt valued as a contributor to the team. Then, in the fall of 2022, the company named a new CEO. The fourth CEO in a fifteen-month period. The new CEO's motto was, "How can we do more with less?" I began to see that the company I once loved was now an organization that only cared about cost-saving initiatives and headcount reductions. This became apparent as our human resource department went about educating the workforce about the company pension plan. I had been with the company for seventeen years, and no one had ever explained or held training sessions to educate me on our pension. I began receiving fliers at home and was inundated with meeting invites to attend in-person and online training sessions. I didn't understand why I was receiving this information because everything I had ever been told about our pension (in almost two decades with the company) was that I could not touch it until I was fifty-five years old.

As more and more people began announcing their intention to retire, I noticed a trend occurring—no one was being replaced. One in ten retirees announcing their intent to retire in November had their positions posted for replacement. I started to see the writing on the wall that, with so many people leaving, those left standing in December would be forced to pick up the extra work from those who left. Of course, this would mean working more hours, and there would not be compensation for basically doing the work of two or more people. I was happy in my new role, but I felt that staying would mean I would be right back in that same toxic environment chained to my laptop, working 70+ hours a week and never having time with my kids.

I turned to God in prayer, *Father in Heaven, please help me to see the path You have laid for me. I want to spread Your light into the world, to love others as You have loved us, and to forgive others as You have forgiven me. Please give me eyes to see and ears to hear that I may live my life for You.* I prayed this same prayer every day, beginning in August.

One night in mid-September, I awoke at three in the morning to what I thought was a dream: a thought in my head, "*Use your 401k.*" I thought this was so odd. *Why in the world would I dream this?* I had no idea what it meant and had put it out of my thoughts until three weeks later when I accepted one of the meeting requests to attend the pension training. The very first example in the training session was about a young woman, fifty years old, who took early retirement. I thought it was maybe a mistake that they used a fifty-year-old. *Maybe it's a typo in the slide deck.*

When the training was over, they provided a phone number of financial advisors that could help answer questions. I called the number and scheduled a meeting with a financial advisor. It was during this call with the advisor that I learned I could, in fact, touch my pension. He explained the "Rule of 55" to me and the consequences if I pulled out my pension money early. I also learned that I could roll the entire thing into an IRA, and as long as I didn't take cash out of it, I would not be penalized or taxed.

I began talking to my husband and telling him I was seriously thinking of taking this early retirement. As we talked that evening in early October, Rob and I agreed that it's nice to have a better understanding of my pension plan, but I was probably going to stick it out and not retire. Then, three weeks later, my daily devotional calendar for my birthday gave me another subtle nudge from God. It was the verse from Philippians 4:13:

> "I can do all things through Him who strengthens me."

◇◇◇◇

In late October, the day after my birthday, I went to church, and a woman, Debbie, whom I had not seen in a couple of months, happened to be there that day. During fellowship, she stopped by and asked, "How are things going at work?"

I told her about all the people retiring and that I had been on the fence about going myself. She and I had talked about my challenges at work, and she knew I had struggled with finding work-life balance in every role I had held there over the past nine years. She encouraged me with full confidence, "You should do it. You will find something else. Do it for your peace of mind and your family. You will be okay."

She talked about a time in her life she had left a job and took time off work. She didn't sugarcoat it and said, "You might have to tighten things in your budget for a little while, but your health and your kids are worth it, and you will be better off."

I kept hearing my inner voice telling me, "Take the leap of faith." Then, two days later, we received an announcement at work that the CFO and both segment VPs were retiring. That night, I went home and told my husband, "I'm done. I'm telling them tomorrow that I am retiring."

I had been praying since August for God to show me the path He had for me, and He had been whispering to me through quiet nudges, but I would not allow myself to see it, or maybe I wouldn't allow myself to believe it. The day the CFO and two VPs announced they were leaving, we also discovered that one of the segment VPs would be replaced by the GM I had worked with for the last two years.

That night, I realized I had been overlooking God's whispers. On this day, I heard the Holy Spirit shouting and finally got the message: it is time to walk away. Time to trust in Him and follow the path He leads me.

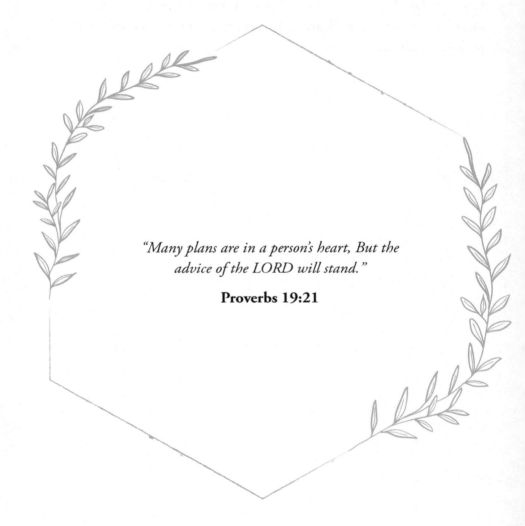

*"Many plans are in a person's heart, But the advice of the LORD will stand."*

**Proverbs 19:21**

# Here We Go Again

T he week after telling my manager that I was retiring early, Bryce was scheduled for his next check-up with his cardiologist. It was November 1st, 2022, and two and a half months from Bryce turning ten years old. The checkup started out as normal: EKG, blood pressure and pulse ox check, physical exam with the cardiologist, and then we were waiting for the cardiac sonographer to come get us for the heart echo.

Once the technician finished taking the required pictures, the cardiologist came in to review and go over everything with me. "Bryce has grown three inches since he was last here, and it is putting a strain on his valve. I would like to present his case to the heart team and see their recommendation to move forward."

I was surprised to hear this because Bryce had been every bit as energetic as always, and we had not noticed a change in him. I also didn't think Bryce would be getting a new valve until he was a teenager.

The cardiologist looked at Bryce. "I don't want you to do anything strenuous right now. You need to take it easy. You can play on the playground, but don't overdo it, okay?"

Bryce agreed, but I could see that he was angry. I asked about gym class.

"He can participate with limitations. I will give you a note for school. And no sports."

Bryce asked, "I can't play baseball?"

"Not right now." Then he turned to me and continued, "Bryce's right ventricle is working too hard to pump, which indicates it's time to either replace the valve or put a stent in, or they may want to try a balloon cath to open the pulmonary valve. He has outgrown the homograft [donor valve]."

I could see that Bryce was not happy about the limited gym and recess and no sports. I asked, "Would it be okay if Bryce goes roller skating as long as he doesn't get too worked up?"

The cardiologist agreed, "Skating is okay." Then he said, "I will present Bryce's case to our team of heart doctors. I will call you with their recommendation in a few days."

I really like the way this hospital used a team of doctors to evaluate Bryce's case. The team included cardiologists with varying specialties, so when the entire team evaluated the case, it was almost like I was getting ten second opinions, which gave me a lot of confidence in their recommendations.

When Bryce and I got to the parking deck, I asked, "Do you understand what the cardiologist told you about taking it easy?"

He responded angrily, "Yes, I understand. I hate this!"

"What do you hate?"

"I hate that I have this bad valve! Why did God give me a bad heart?" he snapped back.

"Oh, Bryce. God didn't give you a bad heart. He doesn't work that way, honey. We don't know why your valve didn't open all the way when you were born, but God didn't make that happen. He has been watching over you and showing us how much He loves you from your very first heart surgery, and I know He will be with us if you have to have another surgery." I gave him a hug and told him,

"I love you, Bryce. Please try not to worry about it until we find out what they want to do next and we get more answers."

⬦⬦⬦

The answer came six days later when I heard back from the cardiologist. "Bryce's case was presented to the heart team, and there were varying opinions on how to move forward. A couple of doctors wanted to try the balloon cath route. Several cardiologists suggested putting in a stent, and the heart surgeon recommended replacement. The consensus is that we have to do something. You will need to call to set up a consultation with the heart surgeon, and he can walk through all the options. Then you and your husband can decide on what you want to do. They would also like you to schedule Bryce for a CT scan."

"Why does he need to have a CT scan? I don't remember us doing that last time."

"The CT scan will show whether his heart has moved behind the breastbone."

I pushed for more answers. "I'm not understanding. Why does it matter if his heart has moved behind the breastbone?"

"They need to make sure they don't hit the heart when they cut through there."

The realization of what he was saying nearly took away my ability to speak. We had been under the impression all these years that the next time Bryce needed a valve replacement, they could go through an artery in his leg and push the new valve through to replace the old valve. I collected myself to say, "So they are saying this will be another open heart surgery?"

The heart doctor softly said, "Yes. The surgeon will be able to answer your questions when you meet with him."

**A**lthough I had made my decision to retire and told my employer that I was taking early retirement, I was still struggling with my decision. After finding out that Bryce may need another surgery, I was again questioning my decision. It wasn't that I was concerned about the health benefits because our family benefits were through my husband. I had lost the ability to sign up for the family plan through my employer years prior because they only offered plans with a health savings account (HSA). Since my husband's plan was a normal PPO plan, we could not have both. My concern was about the co-pays, deductibles, and any co-insurance we might have to pay. Having a job would help with picking up those expenses. Now that I knew Bryce would not only be put through another surgery, but it would be *open heart* surgery, I was beginning to see that being off work would be the best thing for my family.

*I will be able to be with Bryce at the hospital, and I will not be lugging a laptop in tow. I will be able to be home with him as he recovers for six weeks, and I can help him with schoolwork so that he doesn't fall behind. If I was still working, I would be running in to make sure Bryce was okay and had what he needed before signing into meetings.*

Two days after finding out Bryce may need open heart surgery, God gave me another nudge, and my fears were completely dispelled. I logged onto my Facebook account, and a meme I shared in 2019 popped up. It read, "God is still writing your story. Quit trying to steal the pen. Trust the Author." I was finally at peace with my decision. *Okay, God. You have the wheel now.*

Our appointment with the heart surgeon would be a week later. Rob and I were happily surprised to hear that Dr. Stewart would again be doing Bryce's surgery. As a reminder, he was one of the two surgeons who did Bryce's Ross Procedure at four years old. Dr. Stewart reviewed the options the cardiologist had already provided over the phone. He explained the pros and cons of each option.

The most pressing question Rob and I had was, "Why can't you go through the leg as we had previously thought?"

"The donor valve that was placed into the pulmonary position has shrunk. We never know with a donor valve how the body is going to work with it. I've seen where we place a donor valve, and eight months later, it shrinks, and we have to go back in and replace it."

I reminded him that they had put in a larger valve than Bryce needed last time. I asked, "Even though they used an 18mm valve, it has shrunk to a size smaller than Bryce needs?"

"Yes, it has shrunk to 11mm, which is why we can't simply push a new valve through the leg and replace the old one."

He also explained that we could buy Bryce some time and put in a stent. "If we put in a larger stent, I don't think Bryce is going to like it. He is going to feel it because he's grown used to how hard his heart works now, and if we put that larger stent in, causing more and faster blood flow, he's going to feel that, and I don't think he's going to do well with that. Using a smaller stent would only be kicking the can down the road, and we would be right back next summer for a replacement. That would mean two major surgeries in a very short time for a young kid. I feel really confident, based on how well Bryce did with his Ross, that he will be out of the hospital in two days. I may even be able to use an adult-size valve which would set him up, so when that valve needs to be replaced in ten or fifteen years, he can just have a stent placed through a catheter."

We were told that the surgery was not urgent, so it was up to us when we could take six weeks out of our lives to let Bryce heal. "It will take six weeks for the bone to heal and three months before he can go back to any sports."

Rob and I looked at each other, and I knew we were both thinking the same thing. "I just recently took an early retirement from my job, so I will not be working after November 30th," I explained.

"How far out are your surgeries booking right now?" Rob asked.

"We may have openings in December. Let me go ask my scheduling assistant," he said as he left the room.

I looked at Rob. "I know Bryce may not like it, but if we have his surgery over Christmas break, he will not miss as much school."

"And he said Bryce could go back to sports in three months, which would make his recovery in time for baseball season. Not that we have to make the decision revolve around baseball," Rob said, "but he loves baseball, and it's one of the few sports they will let him play."

I added, "I will also be able to help him with schoolwork so he doesn't fall behind. I would hate it if Bryce got held back because of his heart issues. I'm not going to let that happen if I can help it. I think it would be best if we can schedule it while I'm off so I can give my attention to Bryce."

Rob agreed. When the surgeon came back, he had a few dates for us in December. "There is an opening on December 21st, or there is one on December 29th."

"I don't know about the 21st. I don't want Bryce to be in the hospital for Christmas. Last time, Bryce was here for five days," I responded.

Dr. Stewart said it was up to us. "Once we get the CT scan, I will have a better idea of how long his stay will be. If I have a clear path through the breastbone and his heart hasn't turned, placing his aorta close to the rib cage, then I have full confidence Bryce would be home for Christmas if his surgery is on the 21st."

Rob and I agreed that the 21st would be the best option if we wanted Bryce to minimize the amount of school he would miss, but from a kids' perspective, that would be awful because Bryce may be spending Christmas in a lot of pain.

We finally all agreed that December 29th was the best option.

⬦⬦⬦⬦

**I** notified Bryce's teachers of the upcoming surgery and asked, "Who should I talk to about any paperwork needed from the doctor? What can I do to help Bryce stay up with his schoolwork while he's out recovering? He will likely be out of school for four to six weeks. I recently took an early retirement, so I will be home to help with his studies."

The teachers were all extremely supportive and willing to work with me to get Bryce the needed work. Every one of them told me to reach out once Bryce was feeling up to doing work and to focus on his healing first.

With each passing day, I thanked God for giving me the courage to take this leave from my job and allowing me to focus on my family. Knowing Bryce was going to have surgery during his Christmas break and that he had been asking us to go back to Tennessee ever since we had to reroute our vacation there in 2019, we decided to take a trip for Thanksgiving. It would be the last mini-vacation before Bryce's surgery and recovery.

Unfortunately, on November 21st, the Monday before Thanksgiving, Bryce tested positive for influenza A and then shared it with Rob and me. Bryce kept pleading for us not to cancel, and up until Wednesday morning, our plans were still on because Rob and I had not yet felt the full force of the virus. The other contributing factor to calling off our plans was a horrible bout of nose bleeds Bryce had developed.

On Tuesday evening, Bryce called for his dad. He was in the bathroom, and Rob walked in to find Bryce covered in blood. He could not tell where it was coming from. It was splattered all over the walls, the floor, the toilet, and Bryce.

"What happened?" Rob asked.

"I coughed really hard and felt something burning in my nose. Then blood went everywhere."

Rob had Bryce take off his clothes, which were now saturated with blood, and told him to stand on a towel. When they could not get the blood to stop, Bryce held the towel under his nose while Rob walked him upstairs and helped him get into the shower. Even after rinsing off in the shower and running cold water on Bryce's nose, the bleeding would not stop. Huge clumps of blood clots were now coming out of Bryce's nose.

I immediately called the after-hours nurse to get suggestions on stopping the bleeding. By the time the nurse finally answered, the bleeding had stopped, but I was able to talk with her about what to watch for and what to do if it started again. Bryce continued to have those awful nose bleeds through the night Wednesday. He would wake in the night choking, and I could hear him spitting and trying to blow his nose to clear the blood clots. The after-hours nurse told us to try a cool mist humidifier, which I didn't have, and now that I was also sick, I couldn't go get one. I was able to order it online and have it delivered on Wednesday, which seemed to help the nose bleeds stop.

Since we had not planned on being home for Thanksgiving and I had not gone grocery shopping, Rob ordered Thanksgiving dinner from Bob Evans. Unfortunately, none of us had an appetite because of being sick, so we ate leftovers for the next two days. It was definitely a Thanksgiving to remember, but I would not forget the lessons I had learned. Rather than focusing on the negatives, I embraced the blessings of the situation:

- Bryce being sick now meant fewer chances of having to cancel his surgery on Dec 29th.

- We all got to be home all week together.
- No one was so sick they had to go to the hospital.
- Bryce's nose bleeds had finally stopped.
- Reyna did not get sick.
- The rest of my family that went to Tennessee had good weather, so they made it safely there and back home.

Looking at the positives helped remind me that there is a blessing from God in every bad situation if you just take a moment to look for it.

Once the family was feeling better, we decided to take Bryce for a day at Top Golf to make up for missing out on our trip to Tennessee. It also gave Bryce a chance to do something he's been asking to do before he isn't able to for several months. Admittedly, I was also looking for an opportunity to keep us busy. With two weeks to surgery day, I was trying to prepare myself mentally. I prayed, *God, please give me the strength to show courage on my face and not the worry in my heart when Rob and I are by Bryce's side. Please help me to give Bryce the love and support he needs to get through this next surgery.*

I also found peace in a passage I came across while perusing social media. It read, "Don't worry. God has gone before you and prepared the way. Keep walking." This reminded me of the Scripture from Deuteronomy 31:8:

> "And the LORD is the one who is going ahead of you; He will be with you. He will not desert you or abandon you. Do not fear and do not be dismayed."

❖❖❖❖

Surgery day was upon us before we knew it. Similar to the last open heart surgery, Reyna spent the night at Grandma's house as she had a big test the next day at school. Pastor Susan met us at the hospital and was able to come back to pray with us before they came to get Bryce. I recognized the anesthesiologist that came to talk with us before surgery. He was the same man that said he would treat Bryce as one of his own boys before Bryce's first heart surgery at five weeks old. It comforted me to know he would be the one helping with Bryce's surgery today. Bryce would not have any pokes or sticks until he was under anesthesia. This helps kids to relax and not stress out about needles or shots before surgery.

Before we headed to the waiting room, I turned to Bryce, "I have to get one big squeeze before you go because I won't be able to hug you so hard after your surgery." I gave him a giant squeeze and kissed him on the cheek. Then whispered to him, "Remember what I told you; if you get scared at any time, all you need to do is pray. You can talk to God just like you talk to me. He will be listening."

Due to all the changes since Covid, the hospital was only allowing four people to visit with Bryce, so this time around, it was Rob, me, and Pastor Susan in the waiting room. I was providing updates to the family via group chats. The physician's assistant would pop into the waiting area with updates throughout the five-hour surgery. Bryce lost a tooth (they had to pull it because it was loose), and they brought it to us. Getting Bryce onto the heart-lung bypass machine went well. They had told us, "It could take two hours," but within an hour, she was out telling us, "They have him on bypass and are sewing in the new valve."

Bryce was only on bypass for forty-five minutes this time. By 12:30, the cardiologist was out to tell us, "The new valve is in, and Bryce's heart is beating on its own again. They are closing up the breastbone now, and our next update should be with the heart surgeon in about an hour."

At 1:30, we were called back to talk with the heart surgeon. He told us, "Everything went really well. We had to put in a 23mm valve instead of the 25mm, but 23 is adult size, so that will set him up nicely for the future. If that has to be replaced, it can be done using the catheter, and we won't have to go through the breastbone again."

I asked if they had to give Bryce any blood this time, and the surgeon said, "Not one drop. He did not have much blood loss at all. They are finishing stitching Bryce up now and weaning him off the ventilator, so you should get to see him in an hour."

When we went back to see Bryce, he did not have the ventilator in, which made me happy to be able to see his face and talk to him. He was still pretty groggy and said, "It hurts my chest to talk."

We told him he didn't have to talk to us and could just rest and try to sleep. He still had an IV in each hand, a central line in his neck, an ART line in his right hand, a urinary catheter, and the wound drain tube in his chest. They told us, "We want to have all the lines out tomorrow and get him up and moving. He's a little puffy from the surgery, so we have him on Lasix to help get rid of the excess fluid. The plan for the night is to keep him on morphine for the pain, and we are also giving him a relaxation med to keep him calm, which is making him sleepy."

Later in the evening, he asked me to turn on the television but then said, "Everything is blurry," so he went back to sleep.

I asked the nurse, "Why are his eyes blurry?"

She explained, "It's from the medicine they are giving him to relax."

Day two post-surgery was an extremely busy and exhausting day for Bryce and us. During morning rounds, the nurse asked if I wanted to hear what they had to say about Bryce.

"Yes! Thank you for coming to get me!"

As they were discussing the plan for the day, they said, "We want to get the drain tube out and Bryce up and walking."

Flashbacks to the last surgery come to my mind. "If he is going to walk today, I would like him to receive MiraLAX as soon as possible so it can be in his system ahead of time."

I described the horrible gas pains that Bryce experienced the last time, and the physician's assistant told me, "That was probably from all the pain meds he received last time, and he's not on as much this time."

I said, "If it's all the same, I would prefer not to find out the hard way that it wasn't the pain meds and would like him to get it."

They ordered the MiraLAX for him.

I also asked, "Will Bryce be given something to help him with the pain when they take the drain tube out?" I explained our experience from the last time, and I did not want to hear him screaming in pain again.

"He will be given something to help him relax before we take it out."

⋄⋄⋄⋄

The morning nurse hit the ground running and started turning off the morphine at 10:30 a.m. and switched him to a rotation of Tylenol and Tramadol. By noon, she had removed the urinary catheter and told us that physical therapy (PT) would be coming soon to get Bryce out of bed and attempt to sit him in a chair. When the nurse left, Bryce told me, "I don't want to get up; it's going to hurt. I'm not sitting in that chair!"

I told him, "You might feel better once you sit up. The people from PT will help you take it slow, so you don't hurt yourself."

Dr. Stewart stopped by and asked how Bryce was doing. I told him, "He says he's in a lot of pain, and he doesn't want to sit in the chair."

He told Bryce, "If you are up and moving, you could go home today."

Bryce just stared at him without saying a word.

"I think I'm looking at someone who is probably going home tomorrow," the surgeon said, "which is okay. We'll see how you're feeling once you get some of those wires out and you're sitting up. You'll feel a lot better, but if you take your time and want to go home tomorrow, that's okay, too."

Then he told Rob and me he would check back on Bryce a little later to see how he's doing.

Soon, PT came to the room and helped Bryce sit up. They gave him a heart pillow and showed him how to hug the pillow and use his stomach muscles to sit up because he is not allowed to push off the bed using his arms. Once Bryce was sitting up, they helped him shimmy over to the edge of the bed. He had to work his way over again, not using his hands while hugging that pillow. I could see the look on Bryce's face. He was not happy about any of it, and I was especially glad that the PT women were the ones pushing him to get up because I feared I would never have convinced Bryce to sit up.

This time around was definitely different from the four-year-old Bryce that popped out of that bed as soon as the nurse asked him if he wanted to take a walk. Nine-year-old Bryce was now fully aware of pain and its consequence, and he did not want to chance inflicting any more pain than he already was experiencing. When Bryce made it over to the side of the bed, and was able to put his feet on the ground, they let him sit for a bit, and he said, "I do feel better now that I'm sitting up."

"See! You're doing great! Now do you want to try to sit in the chair?" said the woman from PT.

I caught the sideways glance Bryce shot at me like, "Not really!" But they got him standing up and showed him how to turn around without getting tangled in all the IVs and wires still attached to him.

One lady from PT told him, "It will be much easier once they take some of these wires off of you."

Bryce sat in the chair for about an hour. When he wanted to scoot up in the chair, I had to get the nurse because he was also not a forty-pound little boy this time. The nurse needed help to move Bryce because we were not allowed to move him under or pull his arms. Thankfully, Rob was able to help the nurse move Bryce so he could sit up in the chair.

⬦⬦⬦⬦

At 3:00 p.m., the physician's assistant came to remove the chest drain tube. Before they even touched Bryce, I said, "He has not been given anything for pain or to help him relax yet. The nurse went to get it."

They waited until the nurse came back with the medicine. They said, "It works really fast."

I sure hoped so because they didn't give it a minute to hit his system when they were standing beside his bed, ready to pull at that chest tube. Bryce did not scream, and it wasn't so traumatic for either of us this time around. They also removed the ART line from his right hand and the central line from the artery in his neck. Once those lines were out, Bryce felt a little better and could move a little more freely.

Since Bryce still had fluid around his heart, they said we would go home with a prescription for Lasix, which they sent to the hospital pharmacy. So I went to get that before they closed at 4:00 p.m. While I was waiting on the prescription, Rob called. "They are taking Bryce to get x-rays. Should I wait in the room for you or go with Bryce?"

"Go with Bryce."

Thank God he went, because the x-ray technician made Bryce stand with his chest pressed against the wall to take the pictures. Then she asked him to raise his arms above his head. Rob had to interject, "He's not supposed to raise his arms above his head. He has sternal restrictions." Then he told her Bryce could only raise his arms to shoulder level.

She said, "That will work," and took the pictures with Bryce holding his arms at shoulder level.

This is one point I would like to emphasize to any Heart Mom reading this book. You are your child's best advocate, and it is imperative you speak up for your child—even if that means telling someone who should know that a cardiac patient has sternal restrictions and that your child isn't supposed to lift his arms. When Bryce had his first open heart surgery, one of the nurses in the step-down room tried to pick him up underneath his arms. At four years old, Bryce had to tell her, "You're not supposed to pick me up like that." I'm not saying that they are doing anything maliciously. If they are not cardiac nurses who work solely with heart patients, then it simply is not something at the forefront of their minds. They are human. They forget, and it's okay if you have to step up and remind them.

Once Bryce returned from x-rays, they were ready to move us to a step-down room. The nurse had said they had a room waiting for Bryce, so I had already packed up everything and was waiting when Bryce and Rob returned. A hospital volunteer wheeled Bryce to his new room, and as we passed by the playroom, I was saddened to see they had turned it into a storage area. Covid had completely put a squash on the playroom. I knew Bryce wasn't staying very long anyway, but as my thoughts were taken back to Bryce's surgery five and a half years before, I remembered how seeing that playroom full of toys was what motivated my child to get up and get dressed. It made me sad to see it like this now.

Bryce's next mission was to start eating solid foods and to continue drinking fluids since they no longer had him on IV fluids. I ordered food from the hospital kitchen, but Bryce really wasn't interested in eating. The long day of moving him around, having him stand for x-rays, and moving rooms was taking its toll. He was trying to hold back tears as he would cry out, "It hurts so bad!" while trying to shift in the bed to get comfortable. At this point in the day, all he wanted to do was sleep.

The night nurse stopped by and told us she would be by to give Bryce Tylenol at 9:00 p.m. At 9:45, when she still had not come, Bryce was asking, "Where is she? I want to go to sleep!"

I pressed the call button and asked if Bryce could get his pain medicine. At 10:15 p.m., she gave Bryce the Tylenol and Lasix and said, "I will be back at 11:15 to give him the Tramadol."

Bryce was so upset when she left. "She said she's coming back at 11:00 to give me Tramadol. That's the medicine that burns! I just want to sleep!" he cried out.

When the nurse gave Bryce the Tramadol earlier, he said it burned when she put it through the IV. It is a medicine they have to give over a five-minute period, so he winced in pain the whole time she was pushing it through the IV. I asked her, "Why is it hurting him so badly?"

She said, "Tramadol kind of stings when it goes through the IV."

At 10:30 p.m., Bryce was panicking and telling me, "I need to pee!"

They gave us a portable urinal for him to use, and I tried to help him as quickly as I could without hurting him or pulling one of his wires. I remembered that the nurse said she had given him Lasix. Lasix is a diuretic. It forces fluid out of your body, making Bryce have to go to the bathroom … twice!

The nurse came back at 12:15 to give Bryce the Tramadol. I told her, "Bryce is not happy about getting this medicine. The last time he got it, he said it burned really bad."

She used the IV in Bryce's other hand, and it did not burn this time. She told me, "The other IV may not be working right. I will check it when I come back in a little while to check his vitals."

"Bryce hasn't been able to rest all day. Is there any way you could check his vitals now so he can get some sleep?"

So she went ahead and took his vitals and said, "I'll be back at 4:00 a.m."

When the nurse left, Bryce had to get up a third time to pee. After getting situated in the bed a third time, Bryce was crying and in pain. He was also exhausted from lack of rest. I helped get Bryce back into bed, and he finally fell asleep. I lay awake watching him, thinking, *I cannot wait to finally go home so both Bryce and I can get some real sleep, and I can see my son without all those wires attached to him.*

At 4:00 a.m., the nurse returned, as promised, but she had a scale with her this time. She made Bryce get out of bed to stand on it. I was shaking my head at the absurdity of this. *Why would you need to weigh him at this hour? Could they not assign that task to the morning nurse to do when Bryce wakes up? This is why patients cannot get any rest in a hospital.*

The nurse flushed the IV in Bryce's right hand. It was not working, as suspected, so she took it out. Bryce was relieved to have one hand no longer attached to wires. I was thankful to have one more step toward that door to home.

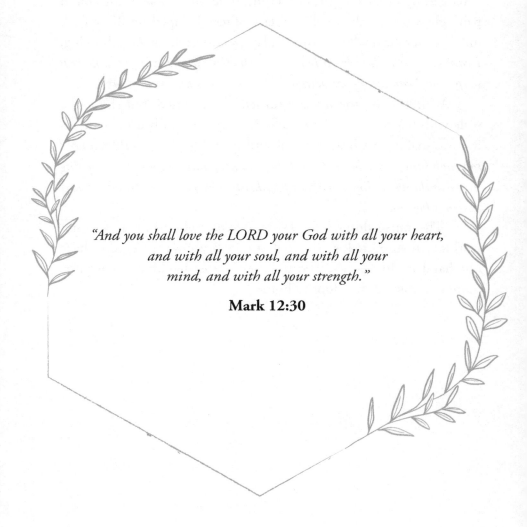

*"And you shall love the LORD your God with all your heart, and with all your soul, and with all your mind, and with all your strength."*

**Mark 12:30**

# 28

# Embracing God's Plan

O
n New Year's Eve, 2022, Bryce got the "okay" to go home three days after open heart surgery. I was amazed that we were going home so soon but also relieved that we could finally get a full night's rest, or so I hoped. The first night home was a little rocky. When Bryce laid down to sleep, he immediately went to put his arms above his head until it hit him that he wasn't allowed to do that. "How am I going to sleep if I can't put my arms up?" he cried. He tried to shift to his side and then immediately turned back. "I can't lay on my side! How am I going to sleep?" he asked desperately.

In the hospital, Bryce had not tried to sleep with his arms above his head or on his side because he was in a hospital bed, and they always had him propped up. He also had IVs in both hands, so he never wanted to move or use his hands with the IVs attached. Now that we were home, he was trying to sleep in his bed but couldn't get comfortable. That night, he went downstairs and slept in the recliner so he could be elevated as they had him at the hospital, except he did not sleep well there either.

On New Year's Day, we tried propping Bryce up with a wedge pillow, but the one we had was for an adult and was too big, so it was bending him right where his drain tube incision had been. My mom brought over a smaller wedge the third night home, and we tried propping Bryce up with it. It helped a little, and we were able to use a few other pillows to try to make him more comfortable. At this point, we were all sleep-deprived and getting a little edgy. Bryce was in so much pain he would cry out, "This hurts so bad! It's the worst pain I've ever felt in my life! I hate this so much!"

The next day, I received a call from the cardiologist asking how Bryce was doing at home. I explained the struggle we had been having with sleeping. She said, "Let him put his arms up."

"Really? That won't hurt anything if he sleeps like that all night?" I asked.

"He's not going to be waving his arms around, pushing or pulling, so he's not going to do damage, and if it means letting him get rest, then let him do it."

"Oh, my goodness!" I exclaimed. "Thank you so much! This will really help!"

The following day, January 4th, 2023, was Bryce's first post-op visit. As we were driving to the appointment, Bryce asked, "Are they doing the gel today?"

I told him, "Most likely, they will." I knew why he was asking; I was worried about it too.

"I hope she doesn't push hard on my chest."

"Hopefully, you will get someone who works with kids who've had heart surgery, so they know your chest is still pretty sore."

I held Bryce's hand while he lay down for the echo. It reminded me of when he was little. He always reached for my hand during his heart echoes as a small child, and I would hold his hand the entire time. It made my heart smile that he still reached for my hand this time. Our fears were quickly put to rest. The cardiac sonographer did great and was as gentle as could be, even when she had to push a little harder to take the pictures at the base of his throat.

The cardiologist came in to review the echo results and said, "Bryce's heart looks great! There is still some fluid around the heart, so he will stay on Lasix for a couple more weeks. The right pumping chamber is a little dilated from working so hard to pump with the old valve, but that should work itself out in time. Bryce's next visit will be in two weeks."

In the meantime, I collected all his schoolwork from his teachers, and after allowing him to heal for a few days, we started our daily routine of reading, math, and science. At first, we took it slow because Bryce was still on a rotation of Tylenol and Motrin every four hours, and sitting up for long periods at the table hurt his chest. With each passing week, the pain tapered until we no longer had to give pain medicine unless he asked for it. Typically, we found that when he overdid it and moved his arms too much, that was when he would ask for Advil at bedtime.

I was grateful he was healing and that my biggest challenge at this point was trying to keep him within his restrictions. It was a good problem to have because it meant he was healing and getting stronger every day.

◆◆◆◆◆

At the second post-op appointment, the cardiologist took a quick look at his heart with the echo. "The fluid around his heart is gone," he said.

I asked if we could stop giving him the Lasix now, and he asked, "How much is left of the medicine?"

"Maybe a day or two."

"Finish up the bottle, and that will be the end of it."

Bryce was also released to go back to school on January 25th, the day after his tenth birthday.

I was so relieved that Bryce's prognosis was all positive and that he was now able to return to school. I was also a little sad because I felt like I no longer had something giving me purpose. I wondered what I would do with all those hours while the kids were at school and I was home alone in the quiet house. The first few days, I rather enjoyed the quiet of the house. After a week, I found myself turning on the television and getting lost, mindlessly watching hours of movies. I felt like I was beginning to sink into a state of sadness. This was the first time in my adult life I had been without a job demanding my time or a child requiring my care and attention.

I began researching online programs for furthering my degree. I had requested information from the registrar's office at two major colleges. Soon I was receiving calls asking me if I needed information to apply. I did not feel that tug pulling me to go back to school. After I didn't listen to God's nudges when He was guiding me to take early retirement, I did not want to make a mistake by choosing something of my will and not His. When I took my dog outside, in the still of the night, I prayed under the stars:

> *Father in Heaven, help me to see what path You have for me. I want to live my life as You had intended. If my desire to go back to school is not of Your will and is taking me down the wrong path, please give me eyes to see and ears to hear. I want to mirror what You taught Your disciples to do: to love others as You have loved us and to forgive others as You have forgiven me. Please help me to learn what I can do to spread Your light into the world and reject the devil that tries to trip my foot from following the path You have laid for me. I ask this in Your name, Jesus. Amen.*

That night I was awakened by a thought, "You should write a book." I was still half asleep and could not tell if I had thought this or if it was part of a dream.

*Write a book?* I thought. *I haven't thought of writing since I was a kid.*

The dream of writing a book went away, along with my desire to be a teacher. I had not thought of writing in nearly four decades. Here I was at this stage of my life, and I had taken time away from work.

*Bryce is doing really well and is back to school now. I have the time, but who on earth would want to read my story?*

The idea of writing a book stirred something in me. I could not sleep. My mind would not let go of the book idea. So, I did what I knew I should not do at three-thirty in the morning; I picked up my phone and searched for how to publish a book. I came across a few ads for companies willing to help self-publish, but I was a little skeptical because they all wanted money. I don't know anything about publishing a book, and most big title publishers want well-known and established authors.

I finally put down the phone, put the thought out of my head, and went back to sleep.

⬦⬦⬦

**T**wo days later, I was at home alone; the kids were at school. I was scrolling through my social media feed when an ad for a free webinar on how to self-publish a book popped up. I signed up for the free webinar, which was being held that afternoon. After the webinar, there was a link where you could request a meeting to talk with a publishing strategist, so I took the leap and signed up for a meeting the following week. I prayed the entire weekend for God to show me this was His plan for me. All the while, I could feel that tug again, something pulling me, driving me to find out more about this self-publishing thing.

I met with a publishing strategist who listened to my book idea and asked me to explain my "why." I explained that I wanted to share my story to help other families that may be finding out for the first time that their child has a CHD. I want them to know there is hope for their child. I also want to share how this journey brought me closer to God, how I learned that it is when we go through trials that our faith is strengthened, if we only listen for God's voice and see His light in all the darkness. If my story helps pique someone's interest and draws them to learn more about the God I serve, that would truly make this book worthwhile.

After my meeting, I was asked, "Do you want to sign up and meet with an author coach for a clarity call?"

I was still questioning myself and unsure. I asked, "Could I take a week to think it over and talk with my husband?"

I also called one of my close and respected friends, who I knew would give me a straight answer if I asked for her opinion. "I think it will be therapeutic for you, if anything. Just be cautious of the scammers."

My husband echoed my friend's concern but fully supported me, as did my mother and sisters. After a week of thinking it over, I finally decided that this time, I would listen to God's nudges. That little whisper in my spirit, that I had ignored, pushed me to retire until I finally heard the shouts manifested by the CFO and two segment leaders, all retiring on the same day. I was finally learning to trust that inner voice. As it says in Romans 8:28:

> "And we know that God causes all things to work together for good to those who love God, to those who are called according to *His* purpose."

I was embracing God's plan for my life. I was not trying to compare myself to Paul or Simon Peter, whom God used to spread His Word. My point was simply that God used broken people, sinners, who asked for His forgiveness, repented, and gave their lives to following His Word. Did they continue to fail? Yes. Peter denied Jesus three times before He died on the cross, yet Jesus returned in the flesh and called on Peter to "Tend My sheep" (John 21:17).

My hope is that my testimony of faith may help others to see what it means to "walk by faith, not by sight" (2 Corinthians 5:7). Stepping out in faith is about trusting God. It is not wishing that He will help you win the lottery or a new car. It is surrendering your life to God's will for you, giving your heart to Him, and asking Him to use you for His purpose. Leaving a career I had invested seventeen years of my life into and not knowing what lay ahead for me was not an easy decision. My faith and trust in God gave me the courage to change my life. I chose to find the path that allowed me to glorify God and all the blessings He has bestowed upon my family.

For me, walking by faith was about walking with the light of God, my Father in Heaven. From the moment I asked Jesus to forgive me of my sins, to come into my life and cast out the evil that seeks to turn me away from Him, I no longer needed a building to worship the Father. The temple was now in my mind, heart, and soul. I go to church to hear God's Word, for fellowship with my church family, and to learn how I can help others. My relationship with my Savior does not only exist in a building or on Sunday mornings. I know God is always with me. As it says in Joshua 1:9:

> "Have I not commanded you? Be strong and courageous! Do not be terrified nor dismayed, for the LORD your God is with you wherever you go."

I will carry His light on whatever path He should lead me.

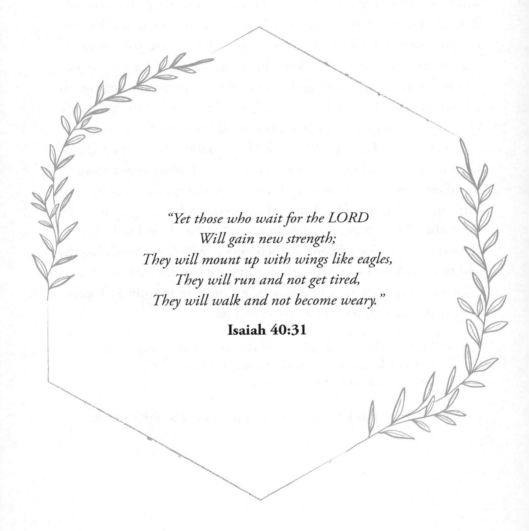

*"Yet those who wait for the LORD*
*Will gain new strength;*
*They will mount up with wings like eagles,*
*They will run and not get tired,*
*They will walk and not become weary."*

**Isaiah 40:31**

# 29

# Living Our Normal

Learning to embrace the life I have been given instead of mourning the life I dreamed I would have has opened so many life lessons for me. I was finally at peace, having laid down the anger, resentment, and guilt I had held onto for so many years. Having let go of that burden helped free up space in my heart to see the blessings in it all. Looking back, I know I am no longer the same fearful, passive person I was the day my son was born. I have learned that when life doesn't go as I have planned it out, sometimes the result is better than I could have ever imagined.

God knows His plan for me. I only need to stop trying to steal the pen from Him. Instead of allowing fear and doubt to dictate my life, I trust in God and pray that He will show me the way. I am getting better at listening to those subtle nudges, and I try not to let them become loud roars before I finally open my eyes to see the glorious things He has planned for me.

I hope the lessons I've learned and shared in this book will help someone else. My number-one suggestion is to seek support to help you through your journey. Whether that support comes from a loving husband, family members, friends, or maybe you have to step out and seek it through a church family. I was very fortunate to have all the above, and with God on my side, I was never alone. Even when I didn't see it then, I know He never left our side. I am reminded of what it says in Romans 8:31:

> "What, then, shall we say to these things? If God *is* for us, who *is* against us?"

I have learned that God was always there waiting for me, even when I turned from Him or tried to solve my problems on my own without Him. In the moments of my life when I felt the most desolate, alone, and distanced from the Lord, He was always there waiting for me to turn back to Him. Looking back at the periods in my life when I was working 60- and 70-hour work weeks, I was so busy working and not living for God. My eyes were focused on the wrong things. When I would reach for Him through prayer, with thanksgiving in my heart, He always met me where I was, forgave me, and I would step out in faith, together with Him, with courage and hope in my heart.

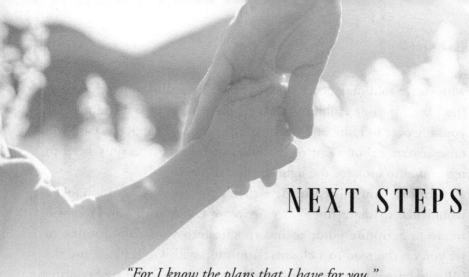

# NEXT STEPS

*"For I know the plans that I have for you,"*
*declares the LORD, "plans for prosperity and not*
*for disaster, to give you a future and a hope."*

**Jeremiah 29:11**

Finding support through social media groups may also be of help if you do not have the support of family. Finding a support group with people who have gone through similar trials helps when you are seeking answers or need someone who understands. I would also encourage you to share your story. You never know when someone else could be in need of hope or encouragement. You may find it to be therapeutic for you as well.

To the parents who are trying to juggle work, family, and life with a child with a CHD (or other congenital condition), I encourage you to remember to set healthy boundaries, focus on what you can control, and whenever possible, educate yourself on the next steps so you are prepared for whatever comes your way. Never forget that you know your child better than anyone else in this world. You are their advocate, and never, ever, be afraid to speak up for your child or yourself. I am here to tell you that God has the final say; He is the final decision-maker. Just because a person in a white coat tells you your child will never play sports (or maybe for you, it's a child who you're told may never walk or never see again), only He knows the plan for your child. When you place your trust in Him, give your life over to Him, and walk by faith, you will surely see God will raise amazing things out of the ashes of tragedy. You only need to remember to look for the light in the darkness.

In case you missed it! As a thank you for buying my book, I would like to share my *7-Day Scripture Guide* with you. You will receive a Scripture guide to incorporate into your daily routine to set you on the road to a closer relationship with God. Please use the QR code provided at the front of the book, or go to 7-Day Scripture Guide ([https://tinyurl.com/7-day-Scripture-Guide](https://tinyurl.com/7-day-Scripture-Guide)) and sign up. I have included this supplemental information as a guideline to start or improve your prayer journey. The reason I chose to include this as a supplement, as opposed to including here, is so you don't have to keep this book by your bedside or in your car with you. While that would be the highest form of flattery if you did, I know that is not practical, and I wanted to provide something you could print or download to your phone to have readily available when and where you need it. Below is a summary of the lessons included in my plan. Each lesson includes a related Scripture or verse, along with each daily affirmation:

Day 1: Prayer of Confession and Forgiveness
Day 2: Prayer for Nourishment of Mind, Body, and Soul
Day 3: Prayer of Thanksgiving
Day 4: Prayer to Seek God's Grace
Day 5: Prayer of Protection
Day 6: Prayer for Guidance and Enlightenment
Day 7: Prayer for Resilience and Strength

Please stay connected and sign-up today for my "Prayerful Warrior's" Facebook Group (https://tinyurl.com/Prayerful-Warriors-FB-Group) that covers information about CHD, important updates, and provides a place for sharing God's Word.

**Website:** https://PrayerfulWarrior.com/

# URGENT PLEA!

**Thank You For Reading *Prayerful Warrior Mom.***

I really appreciate all of your feedback and
I love hearing what you have to say.
I need your input to make the next version of this
book and my future books better.

Please take two minutes now to leave a helpful review on
Amazon letting me know what you thought of the book:

**https://tinyurl.com/Prayerful-Warrior-Mom-review**

**Thanks so much!**

*Tracy A. Ripley*

# ADDITIONAL RESOURCES

## INFORMATION AND STATISTICS

CDC Congenital Heart Defects Data & Statistics

- https://www.cdc.gov/ncbddd/heartdefects/data.html

Types of Heart Disease

- https://mendedhearts.org/types-of-heart-disease/

## RISK MITIGATION AND EARLY DETECTION

Pulse Oximetry Testing Contributes to Decline of Infant Deaths Due to Early Detection

- https://www.cdc.gov/ncbddd/heartdefects/features/newborn-screening-policies-for-cchds.html

Reducing the Risk for Congenital Heart Defects

- https://www.marchofdimes.org/find-support/blog/reducing-risk-congenital-heart-defects

Folic Acid May Help Prevent Heart Defects

- https://www.marchofdimes.org/find-support/topics/pregnancy/folic-acid

## TIPS & OTHER RESOURCES

Feeding Issues for Babies with CHD; Questions for Your Healthcare Team; Tips from Parents

- https://mendedhearts.org/wp-content/uploads/2020/07/Feeding-Issues-for-Babies-with-CHD-with-Forms-070120-1.pdf

Neurodevelopment Issues for Children with CHD; Questions for Your Healthcare Team; Tips from Parents

- https://mendedhearts.org/wp-content/uploads/2022/03/MLHeartGuide-with-Forms-Fillable.pdf

Taking the Stress Out of Caregiving

- https://mendedhearts.org/story/taking-the-stress-out-of-caregiving/

# ACKNOWLEDGMENTS

First and foremost, I thank God, my Father in Heaven, for directing my feet to the path that led me to writing this book. He shall be exalted above all others, and all the glory of this work shall be attributed to Him. Without His love, direction, and grace, this book would not have been possible.

Thank you to my husband, Rob, for standing by my side throughout our marriage and being my rock during Bryce's CHD journey. We have laughed, loved, fought, cried, and forgiven. We've faced tough decisions together, prayed for and celebrated miracles together. I love you for your ability to make me laugh when I want to scream or cry. I cannot express my gratitude enough for supporting my decision to leave my job after seventeen years and for supporting my goal to write our story. There is no other person I'd want in the seat next to me on this wild and crazy ride than you. I am blessed to have you, my husband and my best friend, in my life.

Thank you to all four of our beautiful children: Rian, Kearston, Reyna, and Bryce, who taught me what it means to love unconditionally. I am blessed beyond measure to be part of your lives and love watching the loving, amazing young men and women you are growing up to be. Special thanks to Bryce for never giving up in the face of adversity and providing a seat on your journey, where I was blessed to witness God's amazing grace. Thank you for urging me to find a different job, which ultimately changed my life and set me on the path to write our story.

My parents were the first people in my life to teach me the Word of God. I am forever grateful that you loved me enough to guide me to Jesus Christ, our Savior. Thank you for making me get on that church bus every Wednesday and Sunday, even when I tried to protest. Thank you for forcing me to put on my Easter dress to celebrate the resurrection of Christ when all I wanted to do was wear my jeans and eat candy. As a child, I didn't fully understand the lessons you were teaching me, but now, as an adult, I am eternally thankful that you never gave up on leading me to God. Because of your perseverance, I have learned to have a relationship with our Father in Heaven, to have faith, and to put my trust in Him.

My sisters, Tina, Liza, and Rachel, have been by my side through every obstacle I've ever faced in life. You have stood by me when I needed support, a shoulder to cry on, or someone to listen to me vent. Thank you all for your love and prayers throughout Bryce's CHD journey. I appreciate that even when you were busy with your own families, jobs, and lives, you were always there to lend a hand when we needed it. I can't tell you what it meant to me to know that Reyna was safe, loved, and well cared for when Rob and I had to be apart from her while Bryce was in the hospital. And lastly, thank you for your encouragement and for believing in me when I set out to write this book. I love you all so much, and I'm grateful God blessed me with you as my sisters.

I would like to extend my gratitude to Pastor Susan for your guidance, support, and compassion. Thank you for helping me to understand God's Word and helping me to lay down the heavy burden of guilt that I carried for so many years when Bryce was diagnosed with CHD. I am forever grateful you were with us before, during, and after all of Bryce's open heart surgeries. Thank you for giving up your time to comfort us and spiritually guide us through some of the hardest days of our lives.

Thank you to Jeannie Culbertson for your support and helpful suggestions, which have been instrumental in helping to shape my story to look and read like an actual book. I have enjoyed working with you on this project and appreciate your candor, knowledge, and insightful recommendations. Thank you for your patience with me in answering all of my questions and also for your encouragement. I thank God for leading me to you and placing us on this path together.

# ABOUT THE AUTHOR

**T**racy Ripley is a wife, mother, and stepmother to four children. Her youngest was diagnosed with congenital heart disease (CHD) in 2013. Tracy is a child of God and attributes her strong faith to the trials she and her family have endured throughout her youngest son's battle with CHD. Her testimony of faith has helped shed light on the world of CHD, spreading awareness and providing hope to other families faced with a different path for their infant child than they may have ever dreamed.

After dedicating 27 years to a career in accounting and finance, Tracy made the courageous decision to pursue a childhood dream of becoming a published author. She and Rob, her loving husband of 24 years, live in Northeast Ohio. Tracy finds fulfillment in actively engaging with her community, contributing to the Christian Ed group at her church, and cheering at her children's sporting events.

Tracy finds solace and tranquility in Taekwondo. She earned a black belt in 2019. If she could put the books down and take a break from her writing, she would love to return to Taekwondo to continue her journey of learning and advancing her skills.

For updates about Tracy's upcoming books or to find support in your CHD journey, follow her on Facebook (https://tinyurl.com/Prayerful-Warriors-FB-Group) or visit PrayerfulWarrior.com.